STRATEGIES FOR LEARNING AND REMEMBERING

Study Skills Across the Curriculum

Mary Ann Rafoth

Linda Leal

Leonard DeFabo

Analysis and Action Series
An NEA Professional Library Publication

Author Acknowledgements

We would like to thank the students enrolled in educational psychology classes at Indiana University of Pennsylvania who contributed many creative ideas and strategies to improve teaching and learning to this book. We would also like to acknowledge the Indiana University of Pennsylvania Senate Research Grant Program's support and provision of funds to help in the preparation of this work. Finally, thank you to our families; their support and inspiration made the completion of this book possible.

Print History:
First Printing: April 1993

Note

The opinions expressed in this publication should not be construed as representing the policy or position of the National Education Association. Materials published by the NEA Professional Library are intended to be discussion documents for educators who are concerned with specialized interests of the profession.

Library of Congress Cataloging-in-Publication Data

Rafoth, Mary Ann.
    Strategies for learning and remembering : study skills across the curriculum / Mary Ann Rafoth, Linda Leal, Leonard DeFabo.
        p.   cm. — (Analysis and action series)
    Includes bibliographical references.
    ISBN 0-8106-3048-6
    1. Study, Method of.   2. Note-taking.   3. Mnemonics.
    4. Learning, Pschycology of.   I. Leal, Linda 1950- .
    II. DeFabo, Leonard.   III. Title.   IV. Title: Study skills across the curricu-
lum.   V. Series.
LB1049.R33   1993
371.3'028'12—dc20

                                                                                93-589
                    OCLC: 27677907   ® GCU ~   CIP

The Authors

Mary Ann Rafoth is Associate Professor, Department of Educational Psychology, Indiana University of Pennsylvania, Indiana, Pennsylvania.

Linda Leal is Associate Professor, Psychology Department, Eastern Illinois University, Charleston, Illinois.

Leonard DeFabo is Professor Emeritus, Department of Educational Psychology, Indiana University of Pennsylvania, Indiana, Pennsylvania.

The Advisory Panel

Judy Arnold, Associate Professor and Department Chair, Teacher Education, Tennessee Wesleyan College, Athens, Tennessee.

James Duggins, Professor of Secondary/Post-Secondary Education, San Francisco State University, California.

Thomas Dusley, English Department Chairman, Jennings Senior High School, Jennings, Missouri.

Arlene Lewis Dykes, Third Grade Teacher, Claremont, New Hampshire.

Philip Fast, School Psychologist, Davis County School District, Utah.

Mozella Locklear, Teacher, Burlington City Schools, Burlington, North Carolina.

Rosalind Lucille Yee, Specific Language/Reading Development Specialist, Prince George's County, Maryland.

CONTENTS

Chapter 1

INFORMATION-PROCESSING THEORY AND STUDY-SKILLS TRAINING

"If we only knew how to really help children learn. . . ."
"If students could only learn how to learn on their own. . . ."
"They just don't seem able to remember what we go over. . . ."
"They're in high school, but they don't seem to have a clue about how to prepare for a test. . . ."

To teach students to become aware of their own learning and to help them develop strategic study skills, teachers must be aware of how the learning process works. They also must recognize their role in facilitating this process and be aware of the necessity for changes in instructional techniques across grade levels. This chapter summarizes current knowledge in these three areas.

INFORMATION-PROCESSING THEORY

Cognitive theorists have been able to devise a well-accepted model of how the brain receives, encodes, stores, and retrieves information. That is, for something to be remembered, it must be attended to and interpreted, stored effectively, and easily accessed. The information-processing model (Figure 1.1) describes this flow of information through the *sensory register* to *short-term memory* and finally to *long-term memory* as well as the mental processes that accompany each step. The primary goal in applying this information-processing theory is to explain how children of different ages process information and solve various problems.

FIGURE 1.1

INFORMATION PROCESSING MODEL

||||||||||||||||||||||||||||||||||||||||||||||||||||||||||||||||||||||||||||||||||||||||||||||||||||||

STIMULI

- Visual
- Auditory
- Tactile
- Kinesthetic
- Olfactory

SENSORY REGISTER

Recognition Selective Perception

* Information retained briefly (1/10 second or less)
* **Photographic memory**
* Has no way of determining what stimuli will be of value
* Pattern recognition supplied and transferred to short-term memory
* Recognition of important stimuli in a situation increases with age during childhood (processing distracting stimuli decreases with age)
* Capacity of sensory register does NOT appear to increase with age

SHORT-TERM MEMORY

Encoding Recall

* **Working memory**
* Short duration of 30 seconds or less unless information is actively rehearsed
* Maintenance rehearsal can maintain information in short-term memory for an indefinite period
* Limited capacity
* **Pseudo forgetting** can occur because information decays within 30 seconds after rehearsal ends (and/or other information bumps material out of short-term memory)
* Capacity of short-term memory increases with age
* Site of learning strategies that process information

LONG-TERM MEMORY

- Permanent record of all we have learned and experienced
- Unlimited capacity
- Appears organized
- Amount of information stored increases with age
- Site of learning strategies
- Efficiency of getting information into and out of long-term memory increases with age during childhood

Sensory Register

As sensory information (visual, auditory, tactile, kinesthetic, or olfactory stimuli) enters the receptive organs, it registers briefly in the sensory register. The sensory register holds an exact copy of the sensory stimulus for a few seconds or less. In general, it holds information just long enough to recognize and transfer it to short-term memory through a process called *selective perception*. Selective perception allows only specific information out of the many possible sensory messages bombarding us at any one time to enter into our conscious awareness. It is controlled by the focus of our attention and the set of expectancies we have prior to receiving the information.

These abilities (to direct and focus attention and to set our own expectancies) are examples of the *executive control processes* of the brain (Gagneé and Driscoll 1988). The ability to control these processes effectively is an important element in independent learning. It is also a skill that young learners often lack. Prior to about 10 years of age, children have difficulty attending selectively to important information while ignoring other potentially distracting stimuli (Gagneé and Driscoll 1988).

Classroom teachers can facilitate selective perception for their students by helping them to focus their attention on main ideas and important details and to make discriminations. Additionally, teachers can create expectancies for students by telling them what to anticipate in particular studies, setting up advanced information organizers, previewing presentations of abstract material, listing objectives, and presenting overviews.

Short-Term Memory

Short-term memory is where conscious thinking and processing of information take place. Once information enters short-term or "working" memory, it usually remains there for only about 20 seconds because short-term memory is very sensitive to interruption or interference. Unless the information is important and meaningful or has been actively rehearsed, it quickly leaves short-term memory and is "forgotten" as we begin to think about something else. The material is forgotten because it was never learned. For example, when you look up a number in a phone directory and dial it once, it is doubtful that you will "remember" the number at a later date. You held the number in your short-term memory while dialing. Within 20 seconds after dialing, however, the number was no longer consciously available and was "forgotten." Short-term memory is also limited in the amount of information it can hold. When overloaded, some material drops out of short-term memory.

Over the course of childhood, the limitations of short-term memory become less critical because not only does the capacity of short-term memory increase, but also strategies develop for the effective processing of information in short-term memory (Derry and Murphy 1986). These strategies help to overcome the limitations of the short-term memory system. Additionally, whether or not individual children benefit from instruction in particular learning strategies may be related to their short-term memory differences. For instance, when initially learning to read, most short-term memory space is devoted to decoding individual words. Once a child becomes a fluent reader, decoding becomes automatic and takes up little short-term memory space. The child can now hold and process several words in short-term memory at one time.

Long-Term Memory

If *enough* repeated rehearsal or practice occurs, information may be transferred into long-term memory (our permanent storehouse of information) through a process called *overlearning*. Overlearning occurs when study or practice is continued beyond mastery. Most students learn important, but essentially non-meaningful information, such as the alphabet or multiplication tables, in this way. Many psychomotor skills (riding a bike, swimming, handwriting) are also similarly learned through repeated practice. The key, however, is *enough* repeated practice or rehearsal for information to be transferred from short-term memory into long-term memory. Students who perform poorly on exams often report they are surprised by their grades because they had studied or rehearsed the to-be-learned information for "a long time." What they failed to assess while studying was whether *sufficient* rehearsal had occurred to transfer the information into long-term memory. Once information is overlearned, it remains more or less permanently available.

Many of us used other techniques besides repeated rehearsal to learn the alphabet or the multiplication tables, techniques such as songs and rhymes that placed the material in an interesting or important context. These methods are representative of the second way in which information is transferred from short-term into long-term memory—through meaningfulness. When information is inherently meaningful or important to us, we automatically remember it. For example, we can usually remember the plot of a movie without rehearsing it because the events that took place in the movie were meaningful to us. Young children (before fifth grade), however, often have difficulty with this method because they are often not successful at distinguishing the most meaningful from the least meaningful (irrelevant) events or information (Flavell 1970). Information in long-term memory appears to be stored on the basis of meaning. In fact, the brain encodes information in meaningful ways alongside related concepts and material already known and understood. Thus, it is easier to remember new, meaningful information when we can understand and store it in relation to other previously encoded knowledge. Teachers can facilitate this type of meaningful learning in the classroom by presenting new information in the context of material that the students already know.

Obviously, the amount of information stored in long-term memory increases with age. The most important development that occurs in long-term memory, however, is not its contents or capacity, but rather the strategies that children use to transfer information in and out of long-term memory. With age, the effectiveness and efficiency of the strategies children use improve. This is an important concern in the classroom because most learning strategies are stored in long-term memory, but operate in short-term memory. That is, children transfer needed learning techniques and strategies out of their long-term memories in order to process or "work on" information. The effectiveness (and limitations) of information processing by children, therefore, depends on the limitations, contents, and capabilities of both short- and long-term memory. (See Figure 1.1 for an overview of this process.)

TEACHER'S ROLE IN FACILITATING LEARNING

Teachers have two complementary responsibilities in facilitating information processing: one is to ensure that material is presented and reinforced in such a way that learning is acquired at each step of the process; the other is to teach students how to do this for themselves, how to facilitate their own learning and remembering.

Classroom Learning

All teachers enable their students to remember information by providing opportunities for repetition that enhance chances for overlearning. Effective teachers, however, also capitalize on the advantages of meaningful encoding for retention; they strive to make material meaningful and relevant to their students, which in turn, promotes automatic and relatively effortless encoding and understanding. Effective teachers can take these "meaningfulness effects" one step further by organizing information into chunks and units and cuing their students about important relationships. In addition, they can recommend specific mnemonic techniques to help students add meaning to rote information. Good teachers also engage in periodic reviews of previously learned material with students because research shows that forgetting is most rapid immediately after learning has taken place (Gagneé and Driscoll 1988).

12

These techniques may be very simple (setting the information to music as in the familiar "ABC" song) or more complex (involving systems for memorizing specific types of information such as first-letter mnemonics to remember lists, the loci method for remembering the points in a speech, and the key-word method for learning foreign language vocabulary). Students often retain these specific helping techniques and use them when reminded to do so to retrieve the information in the future. They may not, however, generalize these techniques or generate them spontaneously on their own.

The way in which information is encoded or studied determines how it will be stored and which cues will activate retrieval. This is called the *encoding specificity theory* (Tulving and Thomson 1973). The closer the manner of encoding parallels the demands of performance, the more effective it will be in aiding retention and retrieval. For example, if words on a spelling test are presented in a random order, then studying the words in a random order would be more effective than studying them in the order they are presented in the textbook. Teachers can give cues to their students on the evaluation techniques to be used on new material (e.g., what type of test), thus enhancing students' retention of particular material.

Metacognition

Successful students not only retain and retrieve information, they also monitor their comprehension of both written and oral information and take appropriate action when they find they are confused (Armbruster and Anderson 1981). Similarly, they monitor their own memory processes and are aware of when they have memorized information and can make accurate judgments about the quantity and quality of information they can recall. In the classroom, teachers check students' comprehension and memory through questions, activities, and evaluations. When students develop the ability to do this for themselves (self-testing mechanisms allow for this easily), they become independent

13

learners; they are able to act as teachers to themselves. To do so, they must adopt learning strategies for enhancing metacognition.

By *metacognition* we mean the knowledge an individual has about cognitive processes and how they function. Any aspect of metacognition has three components, *metaknowledge* (for example, knowledge of how memory works), *metamonitoring* (ability to know when something has or has not been retained), and *specific strategy use* (application of various strategies in specific situations). *Metamemory* is a subset of metacognition, and refers to knowledge about how memory works and about how to memorize effectively. The development of metamemory is described in Chapter 2.

Classroom teachers can help less successful students develop metacognitive skills by introducing them to the self-testing and comprehension monitoring strategies outlined in Chapters 2 through 7.

APPLYING LEARNING STRATEGIES ACROSS GRADE LEVELS

Because younger children do not have the executive processing skills to set expectations; to focus, direct, and maintain direction; to choose appropriate strategies; and to monitor their learning; teachers typically play a more directive role in overseeing and guaranteeing these events. As children mature and curriculum demands for independent learning escalate, teachers place an increasing amount of responsibility on the learner. This progression follows nicely the developmental sequence of metacognitive and metamemory skills that emerge during the upper elementary grades and throughout middle and high school (discussed more fully in Chapter 2 of this text). Teachers should assume that young children lack these skills and that their learning needs to be directed to a large extent. As students progress in school, many teachers assume that students are aware of appropriate strategies when studying and are capable of monitoring their own learning to a greater degree. However,

14

while some students may spontaneously develop strong metacognitive skills, many do not. Knowledge of appropriate study strategies, and the ability to choose them appropriately and judge their effectiveness, may in fact separate successful from unsuccessful students more so than ability. Students who believe that they control the learning process through the use of effective strategic techniques are more likely to be successful students than those who believe success is due to luck or natural ability. Teachers at all grade levels can facilitate the learning process by pointing out techniques and strategies—during the lesson—that can help students increase metacognitive awareness. The following section examines how a teacher might do this throughout the learning process at different grade levels.

At the Elementary Level

For this example, picture a second grade teacher planning a lesson on the concepts of solids and liquids. In planning the lesson, the teacher should consider the information-processing model and adapt instruction to facilitate learning. The first step in the model involves *selective perception.* The teacher must engage the students' attention and direct it toward salient features of the concept. The teacher may do this by establishing a set of expectations, by using visual and physical aids, and by establishing relevance for the students. At this level, the teacher will take an active role in directing students' attention, but, unfortunately, may not explicitly outline the importance of listening for cues about what is important. Because young children need such direction, they benefit from knowledge about the cues teachers and others use to define importance. Such knowledge can aid children in becoming strategic learners. When the teacher announces, "Look at the pictures on the board. Some are pictures of solids; some are pictures of liquids. A liquid takes the shape of its container; a solid does not," the students' attention is aroused, directed, and focused on a key characteristic. A teacher might also ask students to repeat directions, and in particular, to repeat the key difference noted. By stressing its importance and suggesting that it be written on the board, students learn that repetition and writing helps them remember. As the lesson progresses, the teacher is concerned with presentation of examples, including both relevant and irrelevant characteristics, and introduction of other defining variables. In keeping with our knowledge of information-processing theory, the presentation should be paced so as not to stress the capacity and duration limits of short-term memory. Children at this age are unaware of these limits and typically do not spontaneously take actions to group or chunk information on their own. The teacher must be aware of this and effectively organize information into meaningful units. However, if teachers overtly note how and why material has been grouped, then students may become more aware of how memory works because this acts to increase knowledge about memory.

Furthermore, teachers in the early grades must instruct their students to review material and to structure the lesson to allow for practice. Study-skill development in the early grades can be enhanced by modeling different types of rehearsal strategies in the classroom. Here are some examples:

> "Let's all say aloud the characteristics of a liquid *to help us remember them.*"

> "Everyone should now make a list on their paper of the characteristics of solids—*that will help you remember them!*"

> "Before we start the worksheet, let's all repeat the characteristics of liquids and solids to ourselves, read over the list each of you made, and then say our lists aloud—*this is a good way to remember the information we'll need to do a good job on the worksheet.*"

Note the importance of making the connection between an activity and its value as a study strategy or its relationship to effective memory and learning. While teachers often make specific suggestions to students about memory, research indicates that they rarely articulate this important connection to students (Moley et al. 1986).

The final stages in this learning model deal with retrieval and practice. To know when and if students have mastered new material, teachers evaluate their students' performance in a variety of ways: through in-class activities, homework assignments, quizzes, and tests. To facilitate retention in young students, teachers should incorporate into lessons activities that help students learn how to monitor their work and evaluate their own learning. For example, teachers might suggest that students check their lists of "solid and liquid characteristics" with a partner to ensure accuracy; to review their worksheets with a model completed by the teacher and make corrections; and to practice the questions on the worksheet with a parent, student partner, or older student tutor in preparation for a quiz. Teachers should also instruct students on how to use the feedback that these activities provide (e.g. "Do my answers indicate that I understand the material or assignment? If not, what should I do? Have I mastered the material? If not, what should I do next?") These practices increase the likelihood that young students will recognize that one can evaluate learning and monitor understanding.

In the Middle Grades

In the middle grades, teachers expect more mature study skills from their students. In fact, by fourth or fifth grade, many children do spontaneously demonstrate more mature understanding of how memory and learning work. Children by this time *know* more about memory and may begin to employ some learning strategies (especially repeated rehearsals) in studying. By junior high school, some students (usually the more successful ones) may have begun to self-test—a very important tool for monitoring learning. Most importantly, students at this age level

FIGURE 1.2

LEARNING STATES AND CAPITALS
THROUGH THE KEY-WORD METHOD

||||||||||||||||||||||||||||||||||||||||||||||||||||||||||||||||||||||||||||||||||||||||||||||||||||||||||||

COLUMBUS, OHIO

Christopher COLUMBUS is sailing to America. He shouts "OH, HI!" to a large "O" that is floating on the ocean.

JUNEAU, ALASKA

"I'LL ASK YOU a question," says a man.
"No," says his friend. "Let me ask you a question...

DO YOU KNOW the capital of Alaska?"

CHEYENNE, WYOMING

Q: "WHY was Anne rOAMING around outside the house?"
A: "Because she is a SHY-ANNE and is afraid to come to the party!"

AUGUSTA, MAINE

A powerful GUST-OF wind is blowing the horse's MANE.

have developed the potential to develop their own learning strategies, to benefit from mnemonic techniques as well as from self-testing. In order to ensure and reinforce these developments, teachers should actively teach students these skills and provide opportunities for practice.

For example, picture a lesson on geography that requires students to learn and remember state capitals. The lesson would be facilitated by the teacher who actively points out important characteristics to students, sets expectations for learning, structures opportunities for practice, and provides students with feedback about their performance. Much can also be done to help students aid themselves to set learning goals, encode information in short-term memory, and transfer information into long-term memory. While students at this age have the ability to generate new learning strategies and to monitor their learning, they may not do so without instruction and reinforcement. At this level, teachers can model a variety of techniques for encoding information, including rehearsal, organizational, and elaboration strategies. Because teachers need to continue to increase students' knowledge about memory and learning, students in middle and junior high school can benefit especially from the modeling of elaborative and organizational techniques.

In this example, teachers might discuss the nature of the task—pairing states with their capitals—and the types of rehearsal that facilitate its learning. (Rehearsal of the paired items in a song or rhythmic pattern may facilitate retrieval). This is also an excellent opportunity to demonstrate the use of elaboration strategies that use visual imagery, rhymes, or other forms of meaningful connection to tie the two items to be remembered. For example, a *keyword method* in which students can remember the capital of Maine (Augusta) is by picturing a horse's *mane* being blown by *a gust of* wind. Columbus, Ohio, might be remembered by imagining *Columbus* sighting land and shouting *Oh hi "O."* Harrisburg, Pennsylvania, might be recalled by picturing an artist's *pencil* drawing a *"harrisburger."* As with any elaboration, the more personal and/or bizarre the image or

19

rhyme, the more easily remembered. The examples are pictured in Figure 1.2. (The keyword method is further described in Chapters 5 and 6).

Remembering state capitals is also an excellent opportunity to introduce organizational strategies. States can be organized according to geographical regions or historical significance. Teachers should also encourage students to make up their own mnemonic devices and strategies because individually generated strategies often work best at this age. Most importantly, this will allow for practice of the strategy and enhance the likelihood that the strategy will be transferred to other study situations.

At the retention, retrieval, and feedback stages of the information-processing sequence, teachers can model self-testing procedures in the classroom. These tactics encourage students to monitor their learning—a critical factor in developing effective study strategies.

One way to model self-testing procedures is to help students develop "study cards" and to provide time in class for their use. As with the acquisition of any skill, feedback concerning performance is vital to learning and generalization. Initially, teachers need to provide students with feedback about the quality of their study cards and the effectiveness of the learning strategies they used on the cards. This is especially important in the middle and junior high school grades when students are developmentally ready to acquire skills for independent learning, but are not likely to be independent learners.

Another method of increasing monitoring ability, is to divide students into self-testing pairs and then to gradually transfer dependence on quizzing done by study partners to the individual student. To further encourage students to monitor their learning, teachers should ask students to predict or estimate their performance on in-class assignments, homework, quizzes, and tests.

In high school, many of the skills described earlier for use in the middle school grades will need to be reinforced. Most importantly, it is during these years that particular study skills need to be generalized and systems of skills such as note taking, test taking, and improving comprehension need to be developed and honed. These topics, along with ways to encourage independent learning within specific content areas, will be addressed more completely in Chapter 7.

Secondary teachers must consider how to reinforce the development of effective note taking, for example, by not only presenting information in an organized fashion; citing frequent examples; and indicating key relationships to facilitate selective perception, semantic encoding, and retention; but they must also encourage students to do the same. This can be accomplished by making specific suggestions about how to record information in notes: providing a skeletal outline of their lessons, and by teaching students a note-taking system (described in Chapter 7). Teachers might also cue students to regularly generate their own examples to test their understanding of new concepts. Again, initially teachers will have to check examples and provide feedback to the learner about their accuracy. Another comprehension booster is to require students to frequently paraphrase information they have read or heard in the form of oral and written responses. It also helps to point out to students that paraphrasing aids comprehension and will help them monitor their learning. While systems for improving comprehension, such as the SQ3R technique discussed in Chapter 6, are helpful in training students, frequent embedded practice (discussed in Chapter 3) is necessary for skill acquisition and generalization.

CONCLUSION

In summary, teachers must think in dual terms. They must ask: "What can I do as I teach to facilitate each step of the learning process?" as well as: "What can I do at each step to teach my students how to facilitate their own learning?" These two complementary processes are essential for effective teaching and learning. They suggest an interactive process between student and teacher that is engaged in thinking about learning in an exciting way. Successful acquisition of study skills empowers students. Teaching study skills and promoting the enhancement of metacognitive awareness allows teachers to take control of the entire learning process and ensures their students' success in the classroom.

REFERENCES

Armbruster, B., and Anderson, T.H. "Research Synthesis on Study Skills." *Educational Leadership* 39 (November 1981): 154–56.

Derry, S.J., and Murphy, D.A. "Designing Systems That Train Learning Ability: From Theory to Practice." *Review of Educational Research* 56, 1 (1986): 1–39.

Flavell, J.H. "Developmental Studies of Mediated Memory." *Advances in Child Development and Behavior* (Vol 5), edited by H.W. Reese and L.P. Lipsitt. New York: Academic Press, 1970.

Gagneé, R.M., and Driscoll, M.P. *Essentials of Learning for Instruction.* Englewood Cliffs, N.J.: Prentice-Hall, 1988.

Moely, B.E., *et al.* "How Do Teachers Teach Memory Skills?" *Educational Psychologist* 21 (1986): 55–71.

Tulving, E. and Thomson, D.M. "Encoding Specificity and Retrieval Processes in Episodic Memory." *Psychological Review* 80 (1973): 352–73.

Chapter 2

DEVELOPMENTAL CONSIDERATIONS

Students at various levels are asked how they studied for their most recent spelling test.
A first grader responds: "I looked at them REAL good."
A third grader responds: "I said the letters to myself over and over."
A sixth grader responds: "My dad gave me a practice test and then I reviewed the words I missed."

Paying attention to what you need to remember (looking), rehearsing that material (repeating items), and self-testing (taking a practice test) are all methods for remembering. For the past 20 years, the literature on memory development has described how the use of these and other strategies for remembering and learning change during the course of childhood. This chapter outlines the results of this research as well as the developmental nature of study-skill knowledge and memory monitoring. It also describes how to encourage more effective study strategies in children. (Chapters 4 through 7 present study-skill suggestions for specific grade levels.)

LEARNING STRATEGIES

Describing good memory and study-skill behaviors is complicated because several factors can influence a child's success in memorizing or learning information. Not only do children have to determine when they need to study, what needs to be studied, and how long to study, but they also have to choose a method or methods for studying. Memory-development researchers have investigated the strategies children use to carry out

23

a variety of memory tasks. Although there has been a debate in the literature on how to define such memory strategies, in general, a *memory strategy* is defined as any voluntary activity that children can use toward the act of remembering or learning information (Moely et al. 1986). Interestingly, memory strategies follow a developmental progression. Research indicates that naming as a study strategy is followed developmentally in time by deliberate rehearsal, which in turn is followed by semantic and associative linkages and self-testing (see Figure 2.1). Monitoring comprehension or one's understanding of material also follows a developmental pattern.

Preliminary Strategies

Even infants demonstrate memory capability when they recognize familiar people and objects in their environment. Infants, however, do not seem to use any conscious, deliberate strategies to aid their memories. Intentional memory strategies have been documented for children at around two years of age. These initial strategies are simple, direct, and require little processing time. When asked to remember objects, the location of objects, or an event, two- to four-year-olds have been recorded using pointing (DeLoache, Cassidy, and Brown 1985), looking (Baker-Ward, Ornstein, and Holden 1984), and naming (Baker-Ward, Ornstein, and Holden 1984) as strategies for remembering. Their use of strategies, however, occurs only when they are specifically instructed to "remember" and when the task or object is a familiar one (Schneider and Sodian 1988).

Rehearsal

Rehearsal is a generic name for a variety of memory strategies that all involve repetition as a method for remembering material. Writing each spelling word five times, repeating to yourself a phone number you just looked up as you prepare to dial the number, and reciting multiplication facts aloud as a class are all examples of rehearsal strategies.

FIGURE 2.1

THE DEVELOPMENT OF
STRATEGIES FOR REMEMBERING

Strategy	Independently Displayed	Example
Preliminary Strategies Simple and direct methods for remembering, such as naming, looking, and pointing	By age 2	Pointing to a toy when asked to remember the toy
Rehearsal Rote repetition of material	By age 6	Writing spelling words five times each
Organization Semantic grouping of material	By fifth grade	Grouping spelling words according to prefix
Self-Testing Methods of knowing when one can terminate studying	By fifth grade	Taking a practice spelling test
Elaboration Creating visual or verbal connections that add meaning to material	Adolescence (or later)	"The meat we eat has the word EAT in it; the other MEET does not."

Rehearsal as a strategy for remembering and learning is not consistently reported before six years of age (Flavell, Beach, and Chinsky 1966). Once children do begin to rehearse material, their method of rehearsal undergoes a qualitative change with age. For example, Ornstein, Naus, and Liberty (1975) studied the rehearsal strategies of third, sixth, and eighth grade students as they studied a list of words. When the third graders (nine-year-olds) rehearsed the words, they tended to rehearse one item at a time (i.e., "desk, desk, desk, desk"). The groups of older children combined the items into rehearsal sets ("desk-cat-shirt-sky, desk-cat-shirt-sky,"). These children also recalled more of the words, which Ornstein et al. attributed to their use of a more sophisticated rehearsal strategy.

Training studies have shown that even children in the first grade can be taught to use the more sophisticated rehearsal strategies (Guttentag 1984) before they are observed using them spontaneously. Although material can eventually be learned using a rehearsal strategy, rehearsal is a rote strategy that does not promote the meaningful processing of information and in many learning situations is often not the most effective strategy for remembering. As older children and adolescents acquire more sophisticated learning strategies, they are less likely to report that they use rehearsal as a study routine.

Organization/Grouping

Organizational strategies for remembering involve reorganizing information into meaningful groupings. Organizing material this way promotes semantic processing of that material, which, in turn, makes it easier to remember. Organizing spelling words for study based on identical prefixes and learning the crops produced in a state by grouping them according to their use are both examples of semantic organization. Although preschool children demonstrate knowledge about similarity relationships, they rarely use this information in deliberate attempts at remembering. By first grade, children still fail to use category organization as a guide for study (Moely et al. 1969). It is not until around 10 and 11 years of age (fifth grade) that children begin to successfully use organization as a purposeful study plan. Children as young as five, however, can be trained to use organizational study strategies to their advantage (Moely et al. 1969). The development of organizational study strategies, therefore, parallels the development of rehearsal strategies, although rehearsal strategies develop earlier.

Elaboration

Elaborative strategies involve creating connections that add meaning to the material that must be remembered. These connections can involve visual images or verbal phrases. The phrase, "Every good boy does fine" is a verbal elaboration for remembering *e, g, b, d,* and *f,* which are the lines of the treble clef in music. An example of visual elaboration is a teacher who tells students to "visualize" what they think a character in a book they are reading looks like based on how that character is described. As a strategy for remembering, elaboration works because it requires children to create connections that have special meaning for them. The first elaborative strategies that children do use, however, are often ineffective because their elaborations are not memorable. In fact, research has found that younger children remember more when elaborations are suggested by the experimenter than when the children produce their own (Turnure, Buium, and Thurlow 1976). On the other hand, the performance of adolescents and adults is better when they produce their own elaborations. These results suggest that elementary school students will profit the most when specific elaborations are provided either by the classroom teacher or in their textbooks or other learning materials. Otherwise, it is doubtful that children will create their own elaborations, or if they do, it is unlikely that they will create memorable ones.

Elaboration is a late developing strategy. Children do not use it spontaneously until at least 11 years of age; dramatic increases in its use occur during adolescence (Pressley 1982). Older adolescents are more likely than older elementary school children to report that they use elaboration while studying. Elaboration is not a universally adopted study skill, however. Even university students rarely report using elaborative-type study techniques (Schneider and Pressley 1989). On the other hand, there is also evidence that children as young as nine years of age can be instructed in the use of elaborative techniques (Wood, Pressley, and Winne 1988).

Self-Testing

One of the last study strategies to develop during childhood involves activity aimed at determining if one can safely stop studying. Self-testing is one way to decide if study activity can be terminated, and this can be accomplished in several ways. Practice tests, looking away and reciting material, and flash cards are all methods for self-testing. Spontaneous self-testing behaviors are infrequent prior to the third grade (Moely et al. 1969). Developmental differences in the quality of children's self-testing behaviors have also been noted. When children initially begin to self-test, they usually do not use the information they gain from self-testing. For instance, a third grader may self-test by looking away from the spelling word she is studying and spell it to herself; she looks back and notes that she misspelled the word. She then stops studying. Fifth or sixth grade students are more likely to use the information that self-testing provides to their advantage. That is, they are more likely to continue studying the material that they missed while self-testing until self-testing proves they have mastered the material. Studies have shown that it is possible to instruct students in self-testing techniques (Leal, Crays, and Moely 1985).

Retrieval/Remembering

Retrieval strategies are additional methods we use for remembering information. If you cannot find your car keys, a method for retrieving them would be to begin looking in places where the keys are likely to be found (e.g., pockets, purses). Retrieval strategies can vary from simple to complex. For instance, a simple, basic strategy is not to give up trying to remember something that does not come to mind immediately (if you do not immediately locate your keys, you continue to search for them). More sophisticated strategies often involve the use of general knowledge, logic, and inference. Knowing that thinking about some related item or event may help you remember what you are trying to remember is an example of a mature retrieval strategy (e.g., recalling when you last used your keys, what you were wearing, who you were with).

In general, older children are better than younger children at using retrieval strategies. From the ages of four to 12, children become more efficient and sophisticated in their use of retrieval strategies when they are having difficulty recalling information. The use of retrieval strategies prior to four years of age is infrequently reported in the literature.

Comprehension Monitoring

Young children are very poor at monitoring their own comprehension. That is, when they do not understand something, they are often not aware that they do not understand it. Markman (1977) gave first through third grade children incomplete instructions for performing a magic trick or playing a game. The older children almost immediately realized that the instructions were inadequate. The same was not true for the younger children; many were never aware that relevant information was missing. Markman concluded that the younger children were taking a more passive approach toward processing instructions; they were merely listening to instructions without applying them. Recent research indicates that developmentally, children understand memory and memory strategies before they understand comprehension and comprehension strategies (Lovett and Flavell 1990). These results imply that children,

29

especially those in early elementary school, often will not realize when they do not understand material or instructions. In fact, evidence indicates that children may "learn" material that they do not comprehend through memorization, but at the same time, they do not realize that they do not understand this material. Lovett and Flavell (1990) use the Pledge of Allegiance as an example. Many young children memorize the Pledge of Allegiance, and yet, not only do they not understand what it means, they also do not recognize their lack of comprehension. This is an important concern in the classroom because if children do not recognize when they do not understand what they are learning, they will not adjust study strategies accordingly or indicate their lack of comprehension to the teacher.

Research on reading comprehension has found similar results. Children often do not monitor comprehension problems while reading. Ideally, good readers would monitor their comprehension as they are reading, and once miscomprehension is detected, they would adjust their reading strategies accordingly. Strategies they might employ when comprehension fails include rereading material they did not understand, slowing down their reading speed, or taking reading notes. Adjusting reading strategies due to comprehension failures is a late developing skill. It is rarely reported in children under eight years of age and is often reported that college students and other skilled readers fail to monitor their comprehension while reading (Baker and Brown 1984; Glenberg, Wilkinson, and Epstein 1982).

SEX DIFFERENCES

Research indicates that girls may be more competent than boys of the same age in elementary school in their use of study and learning strategies (Pressley et al. 1987). Waters (1981) suggested that this developmental lag for males is maintained from elementary school to college at least in the use of organizational strategies. Cox and Waters (1986) demonstrated that consistent sex differences favoring girls do occur across age in the processing of verbal materials and in the use of organizational study strategies. Pressley et al. (1987) found that fourth and fifth grade girls were more aware than boys of the same grade level that they were unlikely to be correct on difficult multiple-choice test items. Boys are also more likely than girls to be oblivious to their past failures as they make predictions about future performance (Parsons and Ruble 1977). After failure, girls make lower predictions about performance. If children are oblivious to previous failures, it is unlikely they will improve or adjust their study techniques accordingly.

The current available evidence indicates that strategies for learning develop at a faster pace in girls than in boys. What causes this acceleration is unclear. It may be related to physical/cognitive maturation, to school achievement, or to other related factors. Because few studies of memory and learning have systematically looked for possible sex differences, those studies that do report sex differences should be interpreted cautiously. It is also important to remember that within a single elementary school classroom there will be variability in the study-skill development of individual girls as well as individual boys.

STUDY TIME

Regardless of the strategies they use, the amount of time children spontaneously spend studying material increases steadily throughout elementary school. Not only do older children spend more time studying, their allocation of study time tends to be more efficient. Masur, McIntyre, and Flavell (1973) gave first and third grade children as well as college students a chance to restudy material for a memory task. Both third graders and college students tended to select items for restudy that had not been recalled correctly after their first study attempt. First grade students were just as likely to select items they had remembered as they were to select items they did not remember on the first trial. Bisanz, Vesonder, and Voss (1978) reported that fifth graders and college students were more likely than first *or* third

31

graders to select items not learned on a first trial for restudy. Taken together, these results indicate that it is not until at least late in elementary school that children make effective use of additional study opportunities. Allocating sufficient study time for textbook material is a skill that is often not evident until junior high or later.

METAMEMORY

The age-related changes in the strategies children use to remember and learn information have been attributed to the development of metamemory. *Metamemory* is a term used to refer to children's knowledge about memory. Flavell (1970) wrote that metamemory consists of three major factors: person, task, and strategy. Everything one knows about oneself and others as processors and retainers of information make up *person factors*. For instance, knowing that older children are likely to remember more information on a memory task than younger children is person knowledge. *Task factors* involve information about how a particular task can best be handled and how successful one is likely to be at it. Knowing that you should devote more study time to difficult material is acknowledging a task factor. Knowledge about potentially employable strategies and their effectiveness characterize *strategy factors*. Knowing that writing down your homework assignment ensures you won't forget it is an example of strategy knowledge. Children between four and 12 years of age become progressively more aware of person, task, and strategy variables. (See Figure 2.2).

As with strategy use, distinct age-related changes in metamemory have been reported in the literature, with older children demonstrating a better understanding of memory. For example, a number of studies have reported that preschool and young children make unrealistic (overly optimistic) predictions about their own memory capabilities, and that accuracy of predictions increases with age (Flavell, Friedrichs, and Hoyt

FIGURE 2.2

COMPONENTS OF METAMEMORY

Three Major Factors	Examples
Person Everything we know about the memory abilities of ourselves and others	• Knowing that we sometimes forget • Knowing whether or not we know a certain fact • Knowing that older children know more than younger children
Task Everything we know about memory tasks	• Knowing that recognition memory task is easier than recall task • Knowing that verbatim recall is more difficult than gist recall • Knowing that relearning something is easier than learning it the first time
Strategy Everything we know about techniques of learning and remembering	• Knowing about and using mnemonic methods such as rehearsal, organization, self-testing, and elaboration • Knowing that use of a strategy can facilitate performance

1970). Flavell et al. (1970) asked nursery school, kindergarten, second grade, and fourth grade children to estimate how many items they would be able to remember before they carried out a memory task. The second and fourth graders predicted their memory performance more accurately than the preschoolers and kindergartners. These younger children tended to overestimate their memory performance. In fact, many reported that their memories were always infallible! First graders are more likely than younger children to know that studying improves learning and that noise hinders the ability to learn (Yussen and Bird 1979). By fifth grade, children also know that recognition is easier than recall (Speer and Flavell 1979), that relearning is easier than initial learning (Kreutzer, Leonard, and Flavell 1975), and that it is easier to repeat the main points of a story than to recite the story verbatim (Kreutzer, Leonard, and Flavell 1975). Older children are also more aware than younger ones that items they just failed to recall on a test are more in need of further study than ones they just succeeded in remembering (Masur, McIntyre, and Flavell 1973). By the end of elementary school, children know that memory skills vary from person to person and from situation to situation, that they do not have equally good memories in all situations, and their knowledge of various memory strategies has increased dramatically from what it was in kindergarten (Kreutzer, Leonard, and Flavell 1975). Metamemory, however, is not completely developed by the end of childhood. There is evidence that many adolescents and college students have little knowledge about some important memory strategies (Schneider and Pressley 1989). It is not unusual for college students to know little about elaborative or organizational study strategies or to have difficulty identifying what's important when studying from a text.

DEVELOPMENTAL DISABILITIES

Research involving children with learning problems—in particular, the mildly to moderately retarded and the learning disabled—has shown their memories to be similar to that of younger, "normal" learners. For instance, children with reading disabilities have been found to lack study strategies appropriate for their age and intellectual level. Torgesen and Goldman (1977) found that second graders who were poor readers were less likely than the average readers to use verbal rehearsal on memory tasks. Similarly, Wong and Wilson (1984) concluded that children with learning disabilities were less aware of how to effectively organize and study prose. Dallago and Moely (1980) reported that fourth through sixth grade boys with reading disabilities spent less time studying and were less likely than average readers to use an organization strategy on a memory task. Moely et al. (1981) found that third and fifth grade learning disabled children engaged in less self-testing than nondisabled children of the same grade level. Results similar to those reported for children with learning disabilities have been reported for children with mental retardation (Brown and Barclay 1976).

TRAINING STRATEGIES

There have been many deliberate attempts reported in the literature to teach appropriate study strategies to those children who do not generate them spontaneously. This research has shown that both young children and children with learning problems can be trained to be more strategic on learning tasks and thereby improve their performance. Research has also shown, however, that many children do not maintain the trained strategies once explicit instructions referring to the training are no longer present. Methods have been developed to encourage children to maintain trained strategies. These methods indicate, however, that strategy instruction is not easy and requires effort on the teacher's part. A review of the training literature also indicates that these methods can be adapted by the classroom teacher in order to facilitate children's study strategy development. A review of these methods follows.

Intensive Training

Researchers have found that providing multiple training sessions so that a study strategy is well learned increases the likelihood that children will use the strategy in the future when not reminded to do so. For instance, a teacher instructs the class to give themselves (or to have their parents give the child) a practice test while studying for their spelling test. Not only should the teacher remind the students of this strategy for several consecutive weeks, and periodically thereafter, but she or he should also demonstrate this strategy to the class and have students practice its use in class until the strategy is successfully executed by the students.

Feedback

As mentioned earlier, young children are often unaware that memory strategies facilitate task performance. Successful memory-training studies have also included telling children that the strategy will improve their performance and why. Let's use the previous spelling test as an example. In this case, the teacher should tell students that a practice test gives them important information about whether or not they can terminate their study activities. Students should also be informed that the results of the practice test will indicate which words they need to continue studying and that they should continue studying until practice tests indicate they have mastered the material. The teacher should also tell students that by carrying out these procedures (by making sure they really know the material), they should perform better on their spelling tests. Additionally, teachers should specifically point out those instances when carrying out a study strategy has resulted in improved performance for students. (After the spelling test, the teacher should acknowledge those students who received better grades because they used the self-testing strategy.)

Suggesting Generalizability

Several research studies have shown that informing students that a current training procedure could be used at another time on other tasks increases the likelihood that the trained strategy will be generalized. For example, the teacher could tell students that not only do practice tests help while studying spelling words, but they also help when studying multiplication facts.

Developmental Considerations

Developmental considerations are also important to keep in mind when teaching study strategies. It would be unrealistic to expect a first grader who is not yet using rehearsal strategies effectively to benefit from instruction in self-testing. The child must first learn how to encode the words into memory before there would be a need for self-testing. Training the child in successful rehearsal strategies, via the methods discussed in this chapter, would be the first step in improving that child's classroom performance. In other words, after the child success-fully masters rehearsal, you can introduce more advanced study strategies, such as organization or self-testing.

CONCLUSION

The results from many studies show that a major difference between mature and immature learners is the spontaneous use of efficient study strategies. That is, in learning and study situations mature learners employ a variety of acquisition and retrieval strategies that are not readily available to less mature learners. These less mature learners are not only young children, but also those children who have been labeled as learning disabled, mentally retarded, or otherwise developmen-tally disabled in school. Study after study has shown that younger and less proficient students are less strategic in their learning efforts. They generally know fewer strategies and have little awareness of when and how to use the strategies that they do know. Children become more active in initiating strategy use in a variety of situations as they become older. Older children also know more about the workings of memory. Improvements in performance can occur when children are taught to use more effective study strategies. However, strategies should not be taught by discussion alone. Children require intensive training and practice in the use of any one study strategy as well as feedback about why and when they should employ a strategy.

REFERENCES

Baker, L. and Brown, A.L. "Metacognitive Skills and Reading." In *Handbook of Reading Research*, edited by P.D. Pearson, M. Kamil, R. Barr, and P. Mosenthal. New York: Longman, 1984.

Baker-Ward, L., Ornstein, P.A., and Holden, D.J. "The Expression of Memorization in Early Childhood." *Journal of Experimental Child Psychology* 37 (1984): 555–75.

Bisanz, G.L., Vesonder, G.T., and Voss, J.F. "Knowledge of One's Own Responding and the Relation of Such Knowledge to Learning." *Journal of Experimental Child Psychology* 25 (1978): 116–28.

Brown, A.L., and Barclay, C.R. "The Effects of Training Specific Mnemonics on the Metamnemonic Efficiency of Retarded Children." *Child Development* 47 (1976): 71–80.

Brown, A.L., and Smiley, T. "The Development of Strategies for Studying Text." *Child Development* 49 (1978): 1076–88.

Cox, D., and Waters, H.S. "Sex Differences in the Use of Organization Strategies: A Developmental Analysis." *Journal of Experimental Child Psychology* 41 (1986): 18–37.

Dallago, M.L., and Moely, B.E. "Free Recall in Boys of Normal and Poor Reading Levels as a Function of Task Manipulations." *Journal of Experimental Child Psychology* 30 (1980): 62–78.

DeLoache, J.S., Cassidy, D.J., and Brown, A. "Precursors of Mnemonic Strategies in Very Young Children's Memory." *Child Development* 56 (1985): 125–37.

Flavell, J.H. "Developmental Studies of Mediated Memory." In *Advances in Child Development and Behavior*, edited by H.W. Reese and L.P. Lipsitt. New York: Academic Press, 1970.

Flavell, J.H., Beach, D.H., and Chinsky, J.M. "Spontaneous Verbal Rehearsal in a Memory Task as a Function of Age." *Child Development* 37 (1966): 283–99.

Flavell, J.H., Friedrichs, A.G., and Hoyt J.D. "Developmental Changes in Memorization Processes." *Cognitive Psychology* 1 (1970): 324–40.

Glenberg, A.M., Wilkinson, A.C., and Epstein, W. "The Illusion of Knowing: Failure in the Self-Assessment of Comprehension." *Memory and Cognition* 10 (1982): 597–602.

Guttentag, R.E. "The Mental Effort Requirement of Cumulative Rehearsal: A Developmental Study." *Journal of Experimental Child Psychology* 37 (1984): 92–106.

Kreutzer, M.A., Leonard, C., and Flavell, J.H. "An Interview Study of Children's Knowledge About Memory." *Monographs of the Society for Research in Child Development* 40 (1975): (1, Serial No. 159).

Leal, L., Crays, N., and Moely, B.E. "Training Children to Use a Self-Monitoring Study Strategy in Preparation for Recall: Maintenance and Generalization Effects." *Child Development* 56 (1985): 643–53.

Lovett, S.B., and Flavell, J.H. "Understanding and Remembering: Children's Knowledge About the Differential Effects of Strategy and Task Variables on Comprehension and Memorization." *Child Development* 61 (1990): 1842–58.

Markman, E.M. "Realizing That You Don't Understand: A Preliminary Investigation." *Child Development* 48 (1977): 986–92.

Masur, E.F., McIntyre, C.W., and Flavell, J.H. "Developmental Changes in Apportionment of Study Time Among Items in a Multitrial Free Recall Task." *Journal of Experimental Child Psychology* 15 (1973): 237–46.

Moely, B.E., Hart, S.S., Santulli, K., Leal, L., Johnson, T., Rao, N., and Burney, L. "How Do Teachers Teach Memory Skills?" *Educational Psychologist* 21 (1986): 55–72.

Moely, B.E., Leal, L., Taylor, E., and Gaines, J.G. "Memory in Learning Disabled Children: Strategy Use, Self-Monitoring, and Metamemory." Paper presented at the annual meeting of the American Psychological Association, Los Angeles, 1981.

Moely, B.E., Olson, F.A., Halwes, T.G., and Flavell, J.H. "Production Deficiency in Young Children's Clustered Recall." *Developmental Psychology* 1 (1969): 26–34.

Ornstein, P.A., Naus, M.J., and Liberty, C. "Rehearsal and Organizational Processes in Children's Memory." *Child Development* 46 (1975): 818–30.

Parsons, J., and Ruble, D. "The Development of Achievement-Related Expectancies." *Child Development* 48 (1977): 1075–79.

Pressley, M. "Elaboration and Memory Development." *Child Development* 53 (1982): 296–309.

Pressley, M., Levin, J.R., Ghatala, E.S., and Ahmad, M. "Test Monitoring in Young Grade School Children." *Journal of Experimental Child Psychology* 43 (1987): 96–111.

Schneider, W., and Pressley, M. *Memory Development Between Two and 20.* New York: Springer-Verlag, 1989.

Schneider, W., and Sodian, B. "Metamemory-Memory Relationships in Preschool Children: Evidence from a Memory-for-location Task." *Journal of Experimental Child Psychology* 45 (1988): 209–33.

Speer, J.R., and Flavell, J.H. "Young Children's Knowledge of the Relative Difficulty of Recognition and Recall Memory Tasks." *Developmental Psychology* 15 (1979): 214–17.

Torgesen, J., and Goldman, T. "Verbal Rehearsal and Short-Term Memory in Reading Disabled Children." *Child Development* 48 (1977): 56–60.

Turnure, J.E., Buium, N., and Thurlow, M. "The Effectiveness of Interrogatives for Promoting Verbal Elaboration Productivity in Young Children." *Child Development* 47 (1976): 851–55.

Waters, H.S. "Organizational Strategies in Memory for Prose: A Developmental Analysis." *Journal of Experimental Child Psychology* 32 (1981): 223–46.

Wong, B.Y.L., and Wilson, M. "Investigating Awareness of and Teaching Passage Organization in Learning Disabled Children." *Journal of Learning Disabilities* 17 (1984): 477–82.

Wood, E., Pressley, M., and Winne, P. "Children's Learning of Arbitrary Facts in Prose as a Function of Type of Elaborative Activity." Paper presented at the annual meeting of the American Educational Research Association, New Orleans, 1988.

Yussen, S.R., and Bird, J.E. "The Development of Metacognitive Awareness in Memory, Communication, and Attention." *Journal of Experimental Child Psychology* 28 (1979): 300–13.

Chapter 3

TEACHING STUDY SKILLS THROUGHOUT THE CURRICULUM

> *Student: "I just can't read this history book; it's too much material, and I never seem to remember anything after I'm done!"*
> *Teacher: "Have you tried anything to help your comprehension?"*
> *Student: "Like what?"*
> *Teacher: "Well, what about the SQ3R technique—doesn't everybody learn that in ninth grade study lab?"*
> *Student: "Well, yeah, we did that in study lab with the workbooks, but I never did it with real stuff."*
> *Teacher: "It might help with your history text. Try it with one chapter and see."*

When students are taught study skills in isolation, they rarely carry them over into other settings. Students need practice in a variety of contexts before they can transfer a study skill to general use. Yet, schools frequently attempt to remedy student deficits in this area by introducing an isolated study or reading lab in junior high or high school. Such approaches usually represent too little too late.

Study skills are usually taught in one of two ways: as a set of learner strategies taught outside the regular curriculum, referred to as a *detached strategy training approach*, or as a set of strategies embedded within the regular curriculum, referred to as an *embedded strategies approach*. Neither approach necessarily leads to study-skill generalization across the content areas. This chapter examines the strengths and weaknesses of both approaches and proposes that the best approach is to combine the two.

41

FIGURE 3.1

COMMERCIAL PROGRAMS AVAILABLE
FOR TEACHING STUDY SKILLS

||||||||||||||||||||||||||||||||||||||||||||||||||||||||||||||||||||||||||||||||||||||||||||||||||||||||

PROGRAM/PUBLISHER	DESCRIPTION
HM Study Skills Program, NASSP, 1904 Association Dr., Reston, VA 22090	Grades 5-10. Units covering various skill topics with activities and suggestions for integration into content areas.
HM Study Skills Program, NAESP/NASSP, Alexandria, VA 22314	Grades K-4. Units covering various skill topics with activities and suggestions for integration into content areas.
Study Skills for Students in our Schools, Hawthorne, 800 Gray Oak Dr., Columbia, MO 65201	Grades 1-12. Guide sheets and specific intervention in general academics, behavior, math, language arts, reading, test taking, and note taking.
125 Ways to Be a Better Student, Linqui Systems, Inc., 3100 4th Ave., East Moline, IL 61244	Grades 5-12. Ages 10 to 18.
Study Smart, Thinking Publications, P.O. Box 163, Eau Claire, WI 54702-0163	Grades 5-12. Educational game designed to reinforce study skills.
Developing Effective Study Skills, United Learning, 6633 W. Howard St., Niles, IL 60648	Grades 4-8. Filmstrips and workbooks on note taking, report writing, following directions.
High School Study Skills, United Learning, 6633 W. Howard St., Niles, IL 60648	Grades 9-12. Homework, reading in content areas, note taking, test taking, reports. Multi-media.

DETACHED STRATEGY TRAINING APPROACH

Detached training programs have been the more traditional approach in the schools. Usually, these programs are introduced at the higher grades and geared toward unsuccessful students. Students are typically taught sets of specific strategies for specific tasks and how to select and use them for maximized learning. The most successful of these programs teach students about cognition and how to regulate their own learning (McKeachie, Pintrich, and Lin 1985). Many publishers offer commercial materials for teaching study skills this way. While most of these packages are developed for the middle school and higher grades, recently, programs geared to the elementary level have also been developed. They may concentrate on a specific set of skills, such as note-taking or test-taking skills, or be general guides for organization and retention of information. Figure 3.1 describes a variety of materials available to introduce study strategies at various grade levels and in different formats.

Teaching study skills through a detached approach has many inherent problems. The foremost of these is that this approach fails to provide students with opportunities to practice study skills with relevant material and in varied settings. Because detached programs tend to treat content as tangential to study skills, students are unable to make applications to specific content, and so little transference or generalization occurs.

Detached strategy training may be effective if students participate in the programs for long periods (one to two years) and if the strategies are taught with content matter of importance and interest to students (Savell, Twohig, and Rachford 1986). They may also be helpful when used to introduce embedded approaches. In this case, a detached program serves as an advance organizer for students. An *advance organizer* is an introductory statement or explanation of a high level concept or relationship that is broad enough to encompass subsuming information. According to Ausubel (1977), advance organizers act as scaffolding (ideational frameworks) for more specific and meaningful information that follows. Faw and Waller (1976) describe the advance organizer as a conceptual bridge between the new material and the student's current knowledge. Thus, introducing the concept of study skills through a detached program prior to skills training within the content areas may be helpful to students. Derry and Murphy (1986) propose such an approach by having the first two weeks of each year devoted to training in learning skills. During this time, different teachers are responsible for different aspects of the program, but all coordinate the same basic principles into their subject areas under a broad planning model or metastrategy.

EMBEDDED STRATEGIES APPROACH

Embedded training programs instruct students in learning strategies and study skills within the context of the regular curriculum. This provides opportunities for immediate and frequent practice with relevant material. All teachers are responsible for teaching and suggesting strategies within their content area and for providing study questions or activities that require particular thinking processes (Campione and Armbruster 1985). Two models that schools might base an embedded program on are Gagneé's Theory of Instruction (Gagneé, Briggs, and Wagner 1988) and Metacognitive Theory as developed by Flavell (1979, 1981) and Brown (1978, 1980).

Gagneé's Theory of Instruction

Gagneé proposes a system of five learning outcomes or products: (1) *verbal information*, representing collections of facts organized in meaningful ways; (2) *attitudes*, representing feelings and values; (3) *motor skills*, such as handwriting and other psychomotor coordinations; (4) *intellectual skills*, representing abilities to manipulate symbolic systems like reading, writing, or algorithmic problem solving; and (5) *cognitive learning strategies*, representing higher mental processes that acquire, access, and organize the other four outcomes in a purposeful way (Derry and Murphy 1986).

Derry and Murphy (1986) suggest that "strategic thinking" itself is probably akin to an intellectual skill and might be taught by using the critical conditions for learning suggested by Gagneé. While specific learning strategies and tactics may be directly taught, an overall sense of efficient executive control over learning (reviewed in Chapter 1) might need to be acquired through incidental learning and problem solving within a learning system that gradually fosters the evolution of these skills. A combination of detached and embedded instruction could create such an environment.

Specific strategies and skills, such as outlining (see Chapter 7), mnemonic techniques (Chapters 2, 4, 5, and 6), self-testing strategies (Chapter 5), and other generalizable study skills can be taught. Gagneé and Driscoll (1988) make five recommendations for teaching specific learning strategies:

1. Match strategies to the processing requirements of the learning task.
2. Provide learner-strategies instruction consistent with students' current knowledge and skill levels.
3. Arrange for extensive practice in strategy use.
4. Prompt students, as necessary, to use specific strategies for learning.
5. Promote metacognitive awareness in the early stages of instruction.

Metacognitive Theory

Metacognitive theory suggests that training methods be aimed at trying to increase what the learner knows about metacognition and learning. Training programs that teach these study techniques and the rules governing their use attempt to develop the executive control function in a direct way (Derry and Murphy 1986). Flavell (1979, 1981), Brown (1978, 1980), and

Derry and Murphy (1986) recognize the following four general categories in such training:

1. building a library of learning tactics
2. teaching students to recognize learning goals
3. increasing the quantity and quality of experiences that lead to insights about learning
4. training students to create a "storehouse" of information about when and how to use learning tactics and their overall utility.

COMBINING APPROACHES

While deliberate instruction of learning tactics and goal recognition might be accomplished through a detached program, it is unlikely that the quality of insight or the knowledge of how and when to apply learning tactics could be gained outside of an embedded approach. Adults may benefit from planned practice exercises that allow them to discover the advantages and disadvantages of techniques on their own, but children, due to the developmental limitations discussed in Chapter 2, are less likely to do so without teacher intervention. To ensure lasting transfer, children should first receive detached, direct instruction and then long-term, frequent practice in context with overt teacher feedback and guidance.

This necessitates a well-planned approach to study-skills training in the curriculum. A school that wants to implement intensive study-skills training into its curriculum would have the greatest chance of success through a carefully introduced series of detached skill and knowledge training programs followed by reinforcement within the classroom. While teaching regular content, teachers can enhance strategic learning in their students through the use of *nonintrusive prompting methods* (Derry 1984, Murphy and Derry 1984). These study prompts are similar to cues that trigger a learning set as described by Gagneé (1980). As depicted in the example at the beginning of the chapter, the teacher triggers the students to use skills taught to them outside the content-based lesson (within the detached program) while learning the content. While making the tactic contextually meaningful, the use of prompts is unlikely to disrupt instructional lesson time because the actual instruction has taken place outside the lesson. This method not only allows for efficient instruction of specific strategies (as noted in Gagneé's work) but also creates and reinforces the incidental learning of the overall skills of the executive processor (described in Chapter 1). Recent work in metacognitive theory (Craik and Tulving 1975) supports this combined method.

Figure 3.1 describes a variety of study-skills programs or training exercises that teachers and school systems might use to introduce and reinforce strategic learning awareness, principles, and techniques at various grade levels. These, in turn, must be embedded in the teaching of regular content to truly effect transfer and generalization and to empower independent learning.

The next section of this book describes specific uses of such prompts to enhance learning for students in kindergarten through high school.

REFERENCES

Ausubel, D.P. "The Facilitation of Meaningful Verbal Meaning in the Classroom." *Educational Psychologist* 12 (1977): 162–78.

Brown, A.L. "Knowing When, Where, and How to Remember: A Problem of Metacognition." In *Advances in Instructional Psychology*, edited by R. Glaser. New York: Academic Press, 1978.

Brown, A.L. "Metacognitive Development and Reading." In *Theoretical Issues in Reading Comprehension,* edited by R.J. Spiro, B.C. Bruce, and W.G. Brewer. Hillsdale, N.J.: Erlbaum, 1980.

Campione, J.C., and Armbruster, B. "Acquiring Information from Texts: An Analysis of Four Approaches." In *Thinking and Learning Skills,* edited by J.W. Segal, S. Chipmman, and R. Glaser. Hillsdale, N.J.: Erlbaum, 1985.

Craik, F.I.M., and Tulving, E. "Depth of Processing and the Retention of Words in Episodic Memory." *Journal of Experimental Psychology: General* 104 (1975): 268–94.

Derry, S. "Strategic Training: An Incidental Learning Model for CAI." A paper presented at the annual meeting of the American Educational Research Association, New Orleans, La. (April, 1984).

Derry, S.J., and Murphy, D.A. "Designing Systems That Train Learning Ability: From Theory to Practice." *Review of Educational Research* 56, 1 (1986): 1–39.

Faw, H.W., and Waller, T.G. "Mathemagenic Behaviors and Efficiency in Learning from Prose." *Review of Educational Research* 46 (1976): 691–720.

Flavell, J.H. "Metacognition and Cognitive Monitoring." *American Psychologist* 34, no. 10 (1979): 906–11.

Flavell, J.H. "Cognitive Monitoring." In *Children's Oral Communication,* edited by W.P. Dickson. New York: Academic Press, 1981.

Gagneé, R.M. "Learnable Aspects of Problem Solving." *American Psychologist* 39 (1980): 377–85.

Gagneé, R.M., Briggs, L.J., and Wagner, W.W. *Prinicples of Instructional Design, 3rd edition.* New York: Holt, Rinehart, and Winston, 1988.

Gagneé, R.M., and Driscoll, M.P. *Essentials of Learning for Instruction.* Englewood Cliffs, N.J.: Prentice-Hall, 1988.

McKeachie, W.J., Pintrich, P.R., and Lin, Y. "Teaching Learning Strategies." *Educational Psychologist* 20, no. 3 (1985): 153–60.

Murphy, D.A., and Derry, S.J. "Description of an Introductory Learning Strategies Course for the Job Skills Education Program." A paper presented at the annual meeting of the American Educational Research Association, New Orleans, La. (April, 1984).

Savell, J.M., Twohig, P.T., and Rachford, D.L. "Empirical Status of Feuerstein's Instruction Enrichment (FIE) Technique as a Method of Teaching Thinking Skills." *Review of Educational Research* 56 (1986): 381–409.

Chapter 4

MEMORY AND STUDY SKILLS IN KINDERGARTEN AND FIRST GRADE

A kindergarten child is shown 16 pictures of household objects and asked to predict how many she will be able to remember when the pictures are taken away. The kindergartner says: "All of them." She then attempts to recall the objects and only remembers six. Next, she is shown another set of 16 pictures and again is asked to make a recall prediction. The kindergartner says: "I will remember all of them; I never forget anything."

The above example illustrates the unrealistic performance expectations that kindergarten and first grade children are likely to display on memory or learning tasks. Although young children do appear strategic (i.e., display voluntary, goal-directed behavior) on a variety of learning tasks, their strategies are rarely as effective or efficient as those used by older children. As outlined in Chapter 2, kindergarten and first grade children's use of effective memory and study strategies is immature compared to those used by older students. This limitation in their study skills appears to be related to limited information-processing ability, poor self-monitoring abilities, and a lack of metamemory information. This chapter reviews the research related to these limitations and also suggests specific methods classroom teachers can use to promote the development of effective memory and study skills in kindergarten and first grade children.

INFORMATION-PROCESSING ABILITY

The workings of the innate information-processing system are described in Chapter 1. Less is known about the information-processing skills of children during the first year or two of formal schooling than is known about older elementary school students. Even so, limitations of the information-processing system of kindergarten and first grade children are evident when observing the study activities and strategies these children use. These limitations hold true throughout the young child's entire information-processing system, including the sensory register, short-term memory, and long-term memory. (Table 4.1 outlines the information-processing limitations of young children, and Table 4.2 summarizes suggestions to overcome these limitations.)

Sensory Register

The limitations of a five-, six-, or seven-year-old's sensory register do not appear to be related to sensory register capacity *per se*. The amount of information a kindergarten and first grade child's sensory register can hold seems to be comparable to that of an adult. The most pronounced limitation that children show early in their school is trouble detecting or paying attention to the sensory information that is most critical for the task at hand (Lane and Pearson 1982, Miller 1990). They have difficulty determining which sensory stimuli should be attended to and processed further and which should be determined irrelevant and thus be ignored. Although this limitation is especially evident during the first few elementary grades, for some children it may extend throughout most of their elementary school years. Miller (1990) reported on a series of studies that describes the developmental progression of children paying attention to relevant stimuli on a memory task. Relevant, to-be-remembered items were coded differently from irrelevant items that were not to be remembered. Children were given about 30 seconds to learn the location of certain objects behind a series of 12 doors on an apparatus. Children were shown what was behind all 12 doors, and half of the children were asked to learn the locations of the six animals whose doors were marked with a drawing of a cage.

FIGURE 4.1

INFORMATION PROCESSING SYSTEM
Kindergarten and First Grade

||||||||||||||||||||||||||||||||||||||||||||||||||||||||||||||||||||||||||||||||||||||||||||

INFORMATION PROCESSING SYSTEM	FUNCTION	LIMITATIONS AT THIS AGE
SENSORY REGISTER	Recognizes relevant incoming stimuli	Difficulty selectively attending to relevant stimuli and ignoring irrelevant stimuli
SHORT-TERM MEMORY	**Working memory** where thinking takes place	Short-term memory span is small compared to older children and adults
LONG-TERM MEMORY	Permanent storehouse of information	Limited ability to store information about memory and memory strategies

FIGURE 4.2

CLASSROOM SUGGESTIONS TO IMPROVE
INFORMATION-PROCESSING
IN KINDERGARTEN-FIRST GRADE

||||||||||||||||||||||||||||||||||||||||||||||||||||||||||||||||||||||||||||||||||||||||||||||||||||

INFORMATION PROCESSING SYSTEM	SUGGESTIONS
SENSORY REGISTER	**Use concrete methods** to focus children's attention: use markers for following along and color coding relevant information.
	Reduce visual distractions by displaying only one example at a time.
	Increase the relevance of material by relating it to children's lives.
SHORT-TERM MEMORY	**Carry out learning strategies** for children in order to free up processing space.
	Review previous relevant lessons.
	Preview material.
LONG-TERM MEMORY	**Relate new material** to information already stored in long-term memory.
	Provide activities that promote **visualization** and **organizational** learning strategies.
	Train children to use **rehearsal** strategies.

Other children were asked to learn the locations of six household items that were coded by a drawing of a house on each door. Selective attention was measured by recording how much study time children spent opening the doors to the relevant items they were to remember (and thereby ignoring irrelevant doors). In one study (Miller and Weiss 1981), only five percent of seven-year-olds opened *only* the relevant doors while studying. Most children opened doors with little concern for whether the information underneath was relevant or irrelevant to the memory task of what they were to remember. Miller and Weiss (1981) concluded that efficient strategies of attention allocation develop primarily between grades two and five.

Classroom teachers may aid children in improving selective attention in the classroom, however. When Miller (1990) decreased the amount of material children were to learn *and* color-coded the doors, he increased children's selective attention to relevant stimuli. Both of these manipulations had to occur together in order to facilitate selective attention; the use of pictorial codes alone did not have the same effect as pairing the pictorial codes with color codes. (Color is a salient cue for young children, and it is one of the first taxonomic categories that children use to organize material.) Making the information more salient to the children's lives also improved their recognition of important stimuli. This was accomplished by explaining the task to the children as a story about what a child had to remember. Subjects were told to pretend they were that child. This manipulation increased the selective attention of even four- and five-year-olds.

Other research has looked at what young children *know* about selective attention. Even three-year-olds appear to know that it is easier to pay attention in a quiet environment than in a noisy one and when one is interested rather than uninterested in the information (Miller and Zalenski 1982). Further, young children believe that interest is more important than noise level for attending selectively. However, it is not until around second grade that children even *begin* to recognize that it is better to pay attention only to relevant items (and to disregard irrelevant items) in order to facilitate later recall (Miller and Weiss 1981).

Improving Selective Attention in the Classroom

There is much that kindergarten and first grade teachers can do to improve young children's selective attention in the classroom. Following is a list of suggestions and activities the teacher can use:

1. Any concrete method children can use to focus their attention is helpful to children of this age. For example, students can use their fingers or a marker to follow along while they, other students, or the teacher is reading aloud. In any subject area, they can be told to use their fingers to point to the relevant part of the page that the teacher is explaining or giving instructions for. Sometimes teachers may instruct students to actually mark critical information with a pen or pencil.

2. When presenting new concepts or procedures, teachers should present only one example at a time. For example, when introducing a new arithmetic concept, the teacher should make visually available one example/problem at a time so that children will focus on what the teacher is explaining and not on previous material.

3. Teachers can color-code important information. For example, the teacher might underline important words on the chalkboard in a different color. All "plus" signs for addition could be written in red and all "minus" signs for subtraction could be blue. Children could even color-code an arithmetic worksheet themselves before they begin to solve the problems. Key parts of spelling words, such as beginning sounds, vowels, and endings, could also be color-coded.

4. Teachers should relate new information to students' everyday lives. When introducing a lesson on recognizing values of

different coins, for example, the teacher can ask children to pretend they are shopping with a parent. Before reading a story, the teacher can tell children to pretend they are going to make the story into a television show and that after they hear the story, the class will be drawing pictures to represent the characters and action. The teacher can also ask students to create a title for the story and their drawings based on the main idea of the story.

5. There are numerous opportunities for teachers to promote selective attention during group discussions. For example, during a group discussion about any one topic, the teacher can encourage children to raise their hands and tell one fact or make one statement about the topic. Before they can state their comment, however, they must first repeat what the previous child has said.

6. To encourage children to listen selectively to specific sounds, teachers can have students close their eyes, be quiet, and listen to all of the sounds in the classroom. After one minute, the teacher then asks students to open their eyes and to name all of the sounds they heard. The teacher can write these sounds on the chalkboard and discuss their relevance to the classroom setting.

Short-Term Memory

Some of the difficulties kindergarten and first grade children have in selectively paying attention to relevant information may be related to short-term memory limitations. As discussed in Chapter 1, short-term memory is of limited capacity. This limitation is especially pronounced for kindergartners and first graders. Researchers have debated whether young children actually have less space in short-term memory than older children and adults do (Pascual-Leone 1970) or if young children have basically the same capacity but use their space less efficiently so that individual items take up more processing space during learning (Case 1985). Regardless of which side is correct, research demonstrating the limited capacity of young children's short-term memory is plentiful.

The capacity of short-term memory is frequently measured by using assorted memory-span tests. Memory-span tests usually ask children to remember in a specific order a randomly selected series of numerals or letters without allowing study time so that the children have to hold the items in their "working" memory until the numerals or letters are recalled. As expected, research on memory span has found steady improvements with age. For example, the average five-year-old can hold about four items in short-term memory, the average nine-year-old can hold six items, and, in general, children 12 and over and adults can keep approximately seven numerals or letters in a sequence in their working memories at any one time. Some investigators have argued that these results do not so much represent a developmental change in working memory capacity as they do experience with numerals and letters (Siegler 1991). Indeed, skills that are not well learned do take up more working space than those skills that are well learned and automatic. For example, when learning to read, first grade children devote a considerable amount of working memory space to decoding individual words. In many instances, a child's entire working memory space may be taken up by the one four- to five-letter word the child is attempting to decode. When this happens, comprehension of the reading material is at risk because comprehension depends on information being retained in working memory for as long as possible so that each newly read word in a passage can be integrated with the words that preceded it. If most or all of short-term memory is devoted to decoding individual words, then previously read material will not be readily available to aid comprehension. Unless held in working memory, material drops out within a 30-second period of time due to the limited duration of short-term memory. Studies have shown that a child's short-term memory capacity does correlate with comprehension abilities (Daneman and Blennerhassett 1984).

Overcoming Short-Term Memory Limitations in the Classroom

There are procedures classroom teachers can use to compensate for young children's limited short-term memory span.

1. To decrease the need for working memory space, teachers can carry out learning strategies for children. When the teacher carries out the strategy, this enables the child to devote the entire short-term memory space to processing the material. For example, when a child is reading and comes upon a word she or he does not know, the teacher can make the sounds necessary for sounding out the word and have the child decode the word. Or, the teacher could reread aloud the previous words in the sentence to give the child comprehension clues about the word to be decoded. In other words, the teacher can provide the young child with the cues that would normally be available to more competent readers.

2. Reviewing previous lessons and relevant material also helps because it calls up material stored in long-term memory and places it in short-term memory for processing. Teachers can review instruction from previous, related lessons, pointing out new terms, concepts introduced, procedures, etc.

3. Previewing material also fosters processing of information in short-term memory. A teacher can preview difficult words or arithmetic problems that might cause processing problems. For example, before a reading exercise, a teacher can identify difficult or new words that students will encounter, have the students decode them, and ask the students to define and/or use the words in sentences. Another previewing method is to have children simply look over the material (e.g., look at all of

the pages of the story or the assignment) before they begin working on the assignment.

Long-Term Memory

Obviously, kindergarten and first grade children have less information stored in long-term memory than do older children. Young children's lack of mature memory and study skills is a prime example of their long-term memory limitations because most learning strategies are stored in long-term memory (but operate in short-term memory). As mentioned in the overview of memory development in Chapter 2, kindergartners and first graders are most likely to demonstrate basic looking, pointing, and naming strategies on memory tasks. They rarely exhibit spontaneously any type of systematic task-tailored rehearsal, organization, or self-testing strategies. They can be shown and asked to use these strategies, and their performance usually improves as a result.

Flavell (1970) refers to these young children as *production deficient*. They have the ability to use strategies, but for some reason do not use them without prompting. Even after prompting, however, their performance is rarely as good as older children who spontaneously display these procedures for learning. This may be because the information-processing demands on the younger child's working memory for both carrying out the task *and* using the strategy at the same time are too great. That is, the child's entire short-term memory space is consumed with carrying out the learning strategy, and so no working space is left to process the to-be-learned material. Even after instructed in a learning strategy, it is highly unlikely that a kindergarten or first grade child will continue to execute it without prompting (Keeney, Cannizzo, and Flavell 1967). Young children clearly rely on teacher and curriculum support in order to effectively process and learn information.

Overcoming Young Children's Limited Long-Term Memory

Following are some suggestions classroom teachers can use to help develop effective study and memory strategies in young children:

1. Relate learning materials to information already stored in children's long-term memory. For example, when discussing shapes, the teacher can ask children to describe items and possessions from home that are circular, square, or triangular.

2. Encourage children to develop visualization strategies for remembering through various assignments and activities. For example, the teacher can have children draw pictures of main characters or events. The teacher could also have children close their eyes and "make a picture in their mind" of the student sitting next to them and ask the individual students to describe what they "see." The same can be done for characters in classroom reading materials and stories. To aid in decoding and spelling, students also can be instructed to "picture" word shapes.

3. Promote organizational strategies by having children verbalize how different items and events are similar. The teacher can ask, for example, how a shirt and pair of pants, a dog and an elephant, Christmas and the Fourth of July are related. The teacher can also ask children to organize materials in the classroom (or even to place fellow students in groups) based on related characteristics. The teacher always should point out the organizational structure of material presented as well as the worth of such a structure.

4. Foster rehearsal strategies for remembering. For example, when learning to spell a word, the teacher can demonstrate rehearsing the letters aloud and writing them several times on the chalkboard. The children can then model the teacher by

reciting the letters as a class and writing the word several times at their desks. When instructing children in rehearsal, teachers should be sure to follow the procedures mentioned in Chapter 2 that promote the maintenance of trained strategies (i.e., tell students that using this strategy will improve their task performance, point out when children's performance has improved by using this strategy, suggest that this strategy can be used to learn other information, such as arithmetic facts, and continue demonstrating and reminding students of the strategy and its benefits until the strategy is overlearned). (Also see MIRRORS section in Chapter 5). The teacher should be sure to emphasize that children must constantly check after *each* verbalization or writing to make sure their rehearsal is *accurate*. It is not unusual for a young child to turn in a page with a spelling word written incorrectly 10 times! Teachers should also monitor to make sure that children do not use rehearsal in an inefficient manner. For example, writing the first letter of a spelling word 10 times down the page, then writing the second letter 10 times, and so on, is *not* an effective learning method. The *entire* word should be written during each rehearsal.

5. Use rhymes and rhythmic activities to help children remember important information. Commercially prepared tapes and records present information about the alphabet, numerals, and so on, in rhyming and rhythmic manners that are easy for children to remember. In the classroom, students can recite their spelling words, number facts, or other information in a rhythmic fashion.

SELF-MONITORING ABILITIES

Besides information-processing limitations, kindergarten and first grade children also demonstrate poor self-monitoring skills. Self-monitoring is the ability to detect a learning or comprehension failure. Kindergartners and first graders often do

60

not realize that they do not understand or know something. This lack of self-monitoring may be because they do not logically understand why they know what they do know because they are in what Piaget's theory refers to as the *intuitive* period. The child's beliefs are generally based on what she or he senses or imagines to be true rather than on what logical or rational thought would dictate. Even though the child can solve problems or perform certain tasks, she or he cannot explain logically the reasons behind solving the problem in a certain way. For example, a child in this phase may know how to count without understanding the meaning of numbers. The self-monitoring failure is that the child does not realize that what numbers signify is not understood. The same is true in any situation where a child memorizes as a way of learning. The child (and others) may intuit understanding because the child can recite information, but he or she does not recognize a lack of understanding and ability to logically apply this information. Memorization of arithmetic facts is another example. The child may work on learning addition and subtraction facts without understanding the logic behind these operations and how they are related, and yet believe that addition and subtraction is understood, or not realize that their understanding is illogical or incomplete.

Another example of a potential self-monitoring failure in the classroom occurs when a child listens to the teacher's instructions on how to carry out a task, says he or she understands, and then follows these instructions incorrectly. Obviously, the child misunderstood the teacher, but the significant comprehension failure is that the child was not aware of the misunderstanding.

Markman (1977) presented children with instructions for carrying out either a game or a magic trick from which critical information was missing. Children were told to notify the instructor if they thought they needed more information. A series of 10 probes about the adequacy of the instructions was used to assess comprehension monitoring, and after the seventh probe, children were told to try to play the game or magic trick. It took an average of nine probes for first grade children to notice any information was missing; the majority had to attempt to play the game and fail before they realized information was missing.

Improving Self-Monitoring in the Classroom

Teachers can work on improving kindergarten and first grade students' self-monitoring abilities by keeping in mind the following points:

1. Self-monitoring failures are common. When children make errors on assignments or do not follow instructions adequately, teachers should probe to determine if these are due to a learning failure or to a comprehension monitoring problem.

2. Students need to be constantly reminded that they may not always understand lessons or instructions and that they should ask questions whenever this occurs. Teachers should also prepare a large number of learning probes and checks to assess student understanding of new concepts and directions.

3. Teachers can use activities in the classroom to stimulate self-monitoring awareness. For example, the teacher can tell students that she or he is going to be telling a story, reading a story, or giving instructions and that some important piece of information is lacking. Students must determine what information they need. If children have difficulty with this task, the teacher should instruct children to try to mentally carry out the actions or task in their heads to see at what point the activity becomes impossible to complete. If this is not successful in promoting self-monitoring, the teacher (or student) should try to physically act out the instructions.

4. Teachers can ask students to describe situations when they did not understand someone or something. They should also relate what they did in that situation and what they should have done. The teacher may want to first model this for the

children with a personal experience of misunderstanding. Children can even role play these situations.

METAMEMORY

Kindergarten and first grade children have limited knowledge about person, task, and strategy factors (described in Chapter 2) related to knowledge about memory and learning. Part of their limited metamemory is related to unrealistic person and task predictions and overconfidence in their own abilities. For example, when Kreutzer, Leonard, and Flavell (1975) asked children if they ever forgot things, 30 percent of the kindergarten children asserted that they never forgot anything. Five- and six-year-olds also tend to overestimate their performance on memory tasks (Worden and Sladewski-Awig 1982). Kindergarten and first grade children also have difficulty in determining when to stop studying or in estimating their recall readiness. Flavell, Friedrichs, and Hoyt (1970) asked children to study material until they were absolutely certain they would be able to recall the entire list without error. Although kindergartners and first graders declared that they could recall the list perfectly, they usually did not. Even after young children experience failure and do not recall all of the material, they do not lower their subsequent recall predictions but continue to overestimate their future recall performance (Levin et al. 1971). Kindergarten and first grade children also have limited knowledge about many memory and study strategies. They are usually unaware that strategies such as organization and rehearsal are more effective than merely looking and renaming (Justice 1985 and Pascual-Leone 1970).

Improving Metamemory in the Classroom

Classroom teachers can help develop metamemory and various memory strategies. A few suggestions follow.

1. When instructing children in a learning or memory strategy or requiring them to use that strategy, point out that the reason they should use the strategy is because it is useful and it will improve their performance. Examples: "Saying our spelling words aloud will help us remember"; "Repeating our math facts is a good way to remember"; "Checking with a partner is a good way to see if your answer is right!"

2. Whenever a student's performance improves because of the use of a study or learning strategy that either was instructed or that the child used spontaneously, immediately point out this improvement to the child.

3. Talk to children about forgetting and point out that everyone forgets at some time or another. The teacher can provide examples and ask the students to relate when someone they know has forgotten and when they themselves have forgotten. The teacher can then ask students for suggestions to help prevent forgetting.

CONCLUSION

Although kindergarten and first grade children are limited in their information-processing skills, they can achieve with a teacher who is aware of these limitations and provides a learning environment that capitalizes on students' strengths.

REFERENCES

Case, R. *Intellectual Development: Birth to Adulthood.* Orlando, Fla.: Academic Press, 1985.

Daneman, M., and Blennerhassett, A. "How to Assess the Listening Comprehension Skills of Prereaders." *Journal of Educational Psychology* 76 (1984): 1372–81.

Flavell, J.H. "Developmental Studies of Mediated Memory." In *Advances in Child Development and Behavior,* edited by H.W. Reese and L.P. Lipsitt. New York: Academic Press, 1970.

Flavell, J.H., Friedrichs, A.G., and Hoyt, J.D. "Developmental Changes in Memorization Processes." *Cognitive Psychology* 1 (1970): 324–40.

Justice, E.M. "Categorization as a Preferred Memory Strategy: Developmental Changes During Elementary School." *Developmental Psychology* 21 (1985): 1105–10.

Keeney, F.J., Cannizzo, S.R., and Flavell, J.H. "Spontaneous and Induced Verbal Rehearsal in a Recall Task." *Child Development* 38 (1967): 953–66.

Kreutzer, M.A., Leonard, C., and Flavell, J.H. "An Interview Study of Children's Knowledge About Memory." *Monographs of the Society for Research in Child Development* 40 (1, Serial No. 159): 1975.

Lane, D.M., and Pearson, D.A. "The Development of Selective Attention." *Merrill-Palmer Quarterly* 28 (1982): 317–37.

Levin, J.R., Yussen, S.R., DeRose, T.M., and Pressley, M. "Developmental Changes in Assessing Recall and Recognition Memory Capacity." *Developmental Psychology* 11 (1971): 608–15.

Markman, E.M. "Realizing That You Don't Understand: A Preliminary Investigation." *Child Development* 48 (1977): 986–92.

Miller, P.H. "The Development of Strategies of Selective Attention." In *Children's Strategies: Contemporary Views of Cognitive Development*, edited by D.F. Bjorklund. Hillside, N.J.: Lawrence Erlbaum, 1990.

Miller, P.H., and Weiss, M.G. "Children's Attention Allocation, Understanding of Attention, and Performance on the Incidental Learning Task." *Child Development* 52 (1981): 1183–90.

Miller, P.H., and Weiss, M.G. "Children's and Adult's Knowledge About What Variables Affect Selective Attention." *Child Development* 53 (1982): 543–49.

Miller, P.H., and Zalenski, R. "Preschoolers' Knowledge About Attention." *Developmental Psychology* 18 (1982): 871–75.

Pascual-Leone, J. "A Mathematical Model for the Transition Rule in Piaget's Developmental Stages." *Acta Psychologia* 63 (1970): 301–45.

Schneider, W. "The Role of Conceptual Knowledge and Metamemory in the Development of Organizational Processes in Memory." *Journal of Experimental Child Psychology* 42 (1986): 318–36.

Siegler, R.S. *Children's Thinking* (2nd ed.). Englewood Cliffs, N.J.: Prentice Hall, 1991.

Worden, P.E., and Sladewski-Awig, L.J. "Children's Awareness of Memorability." *Journal of Educational Psychology* 74 (1982): 341–50.

Chapter 5

MEMORY AND STUDY SKILLS IN THE ELEMENTARY GRADES

During the elementary school years, children grow enormously in their knowledge of memory and cognitive processes.

For example: Children watch two different video tapes of a child studying for a memory task. The material the child is studying consists of 25 pictures of objects that belong to five conceptual categories (five animals, five plants, five clothing items, five furniture items, and five people). In one video tape, the child looks at and names all of the pictures. In the other tape, the child arranges the items into conceptual categories before he or she recites the names of the items. Children are asked which method is the more effective study technique.

A second grader replies: "It doesn't matter. They're both good."

A fifth grader responds: "When you group the pictures together, it's better."

Not only what children know but also how they actually study and carry out various learning activities becomes more strategic during the elementary school years. Their information-processing abilities also improve during this time. Children become increasingly able to recognize what is important in learning and study situations, their short-term memory span increases by one or two items, and they store more and more information about study strategies into their long-term memories. Classroom teachers can do much to foster this development and to ensure that students acquire effective strategies during this critical phase of study-skill development. This chapter begins by outlining

67

relevant changes in children's memory strategies during elementary school and then presents information and strategy suggestions related to specific content areas.

MEMORY IN THE ELEMENTARY GRADES

What children do when they are required to remember or study material changes markedly during the course of the elementary grades two through six. Memory researchers report that between the ages of seven and 10 a transition occurs wherein children appear aware that each learning task requires some activity or effort (Schneider 1988) although they often do not use an effective strategy for the task. It is not until around 10 years of age (fifth grade) that some children spontaneously display mature strategy efforts on a variety of memory tasks.

For example, there is a gradual refinement of rehearsal skills during the elementary grades. Single-item rehearsal is gradually replaced by cumulative rehearsal (rehearsing several items at one time.) Eight-year-olds usually rehearse one, or at the most, two items per rehearsal set; by 10 years of age, children are rehearsing three or four items at a time (Palincsar 1986). Guttantag (1985) found that young children do not use cumulative rehearsal spontaneously because it requires too much mental effort to do so; working on several items at one time in short-term memory tends to overload their information-processing capacities. Young children, however, can be trained to use cumulative rehearsal effectively, and their recall will improve as a result (McShane 1991).

Organizational study strategies (semantic grouping of related items) usually develop later than cumulative rehearsal. Children do not spontaneously use organizational methods effectively until around 10 to 11 years of age (Moely et al. 1969). As with cumulative rehearsal, even second grade children can improve their performance by being instructed to use organizational strategies during study (Kee and Bell 1981).

Rudimentary self-testing strategies are first evident at around the second and third grade, but it is not until the fifth and sixth grades that children can use self-testing to effectively determine when they can terminate studying. Young children, however, can be trained to make better use of self-testing than they do (Leal, Crays, and Moely 1985).

Theorists have speculated that many of these memory skills develop or are learned because of the emphasis that formal schooling places on memory. Not all children acquire these skills, however. Those who do not, find themselves at an educational disadvantage. Many times these students fail, not because of a lack of intelligence, but rather from a lack of appropriate learning and study strategies. When environmental support is provided for the implementation of a strategy through: (1) instructional materials and (2) a teacher who demonstrates learning strategies and an appreciation for them, even very young children and children with learning problems exhibit spontaneous strategy use. With practice, these strategies can become more automatic.

To implement learning strategies, beginning students require both favorable processing conditions and learning materials. With experience and age, they are able to carry these strategies over into less favorable conditions. The classroom provides many opportunities for teachers to present strategy instruction to children. They can teach them as part of the regular curriculum without buying special material or supplies. Strategies can also be presented in a game context, which is particularly effective for children of this age. Strategies should never be taught by discussion alone. Ghatala, Levin, Pressley, and Goodwin, (1986) found that young grade school children had to be *explicitly* taught how to compare performance produced by different strategies, how to attribute performance to strategy use, and how to decide what strategy to use.

Unfortunately, as pointed out by Pressley et al. (1989), there is little evidence that teachers actively teach learning strategies for reading comprehension, mathematical problem solving, or memorization. The remainder of this chapter describes methods that elementary teachers can use to promote strategy use in these subject areas.

ENCOURAGING STRATEGY USE IN THE ELEMENTARY CLASSROOM

As outlined in Chapter 2, strategy instruction requires:

1. direct explanation on how to carry out the strategy
2. information on when and where to use it
3. specific modeling of the strategy by the teacher by using concrete examples
4. plenty of practice by students
5. continual feedback from the teacher about the strategy's effectiveness and the students'effectiveness in carrying out the strategy.

Figure 5.1 presents a mnemonic method (the MIRRORS model) for teaching strategies effectively. When using this, or any other method, students should not be left on their own to determine what strategy is useful on any one learning task, but should be specifically prompted when to use what strategy.

Because not all strategies are enjoyable to carry out and they usually require effort, it is crucial that students understand the benefits of strategies. Students must come to believe that strategies are useful and good and are worth the additional time and effort they require in learning situations. If they believe the effort that strategies require pays off by increasing their task performance, they are more likely to use strategies spontaneously. Because young children often fail to monitor the effectiveness of strategies when they do use them, teachers need to point out continually how the use of strategies is improving students' classroom performance.

Strategy Instruction in Reading

Reading is perhaps the most important skill that children learn in the elementary classroom. The key to success in early

FIGURE 5.1

M-I-R-R-O-R-S: TEACHING STRATEGY
USE EFFECTIVELY

|||||||||||||||||||||||||||||||||||||||||||||||||||||||||||||||||||||||||||||||||||||||||||||||||||||||||||

Remember, children's failure to use a study strategy is often
due to an instructional failure rather than a learning failure.

GOOD STRATEGY INSTRUCTION INCLUDES:

- Direct **explanation** and **modeling** of the strategy

- Information on **when** and **how** to use it

- **Reminders** to use the strategy

- Repeated use of the **strategy**

- Constant **feedback** about the strategy's usefulness

- Constant **feedback** about the student's improved
  performance when he or she uses the strategy

- **Generalizing** the **strategy** to other learning tasks

A HELPFUL MNEMONIC: **M-I-R-R-O-R-S**

M - Model the strategy; explain how to carry it out

I - Inform the students about when and how to use it

R - Remind them to use the strategy

R - Repeat the strategy: practice, practice, practice

O - Outline the strategy's usefulness via constant feedback

R - Reassess the student's performance as a result of using
     the strategy

S - Stress strategy generalization

reading development is the identification of individual words. Children use two possible word identification procedures while reading. One is *phonological recording,* or "sounding out" the word. The other is when the child *retrieves* the word from long-term memory without having to phonologically decode it (sight-word method). While reading, children first try to use retrieval, and when retrieval fails, they rely on sounding out the word (Siegler 1991). Children become able to retrieve more and more words because repeated phonological decoding causes individual words to eventually be stored in long-term memory (Jorm and Share 1983). These two methods of word identification are related to the two main approaches that have been used to teach children to read—the *whole-word approach* (teaching visual retrieval) and the *phonetic approach* (teaching phonological decoding or phonics). Because phonics-based instruction teaches children methods for identifying unfamiliar words, and thus allows them to be independent readers, many researchers feel that it is superior to the whole-word approach (Lesgold and Perfetti 1981).

Poor readers seem to have difficulty establishing phonological representations for words. This may be the result of a delay in the acquisition of phonological codes (Olson et al. 1984) and/or because of phonetic confusions (Morais et al. 1979). The following are strategies to help children decode words while reading.

1. Addition/Subtraction Game: This addition and subtraction game can increase children's awareness of phonological sounds (Olson et al. 1984). The game requires children to respond to the effects of adding and removing letters from individual words. For example, the teacher can ask children: "What would the word *sand* sound like if we added a *t* to it?"(Children answer: "Stand.") Or, the teacher can ask: "What would the word *sand* sound like if we removed the *n*?" (Children answer: "Sad.") Children can even play as teams, and each team can compose its own addition and subtraction

72

problems. Children can use words they encounter in their reading as well as those in other subject areas (e.g., social studies, spelling) as the base words for some of the problems.

2. Phonetic Organization: Another activity children can engage in to increase their awareness of the phonological representation of words is one that requires them to organize or group words according to sounds. Words can be grouped according to their beginning, vowel, prefix, or suffix sounds. Words to be grouped can be vocabulary words, spelling words, or words in a paragraph that children are reading. Children can work in pairs and recite the words to one another and discuss the sounds they hear.

Early reading research focused on studying children's decoding of printed material, but current research is concerned with text processing, prose memory, and reading comprehension (Hall 1989). This shift in interest came about when researchers realized that the ability to decode individual words does not guarantee comprehension of what is read. Children must not only identify individual words while reading, they must also learn how to relate a given word to the overall meaning of a sentence and the sentence to the overall meaning of the text. Research has so far indicated that reading to understand is hard work (Daneman and Green 1986), and although no single text processing strategy works in all reading situations, *the skilled reader is strategic while reading.*

Age, reading experience, and information-processing capabilities all influence how strategic a given child will be while reading. For example, the information-processing abilities of an individual child sets limits on the amount of text a child can see in a given eye fixation, the amount of information that the child can hold in short-term memory, and how quickly information can be retrieved from long-term memory. Research shows that an increase in short-term memory span is related to an increase in children's reading comprehension abilities because this increase in working memory space allows children to integrate previous information with new ideas and to make connections between them (Daneman and Carpenter 1980).

A major problem that young and less skilled readers have while reading is that they often do not engage in comprehension monitoring while reading. That is, they do not notice that they do not understand what they are reading. For example, Markman (1979) presented reading material that contained major discrepancies and nonsensical information to third, fifth, and sixth grade students. Nearly half of the children at each grade level did not detect these errors. Skilled reading comprehension and comprehension monitoring rely on fluent word decoding and processing, practice, and instruction (Beck and McKeown 1986). Reciprocal teaching and cooperative learning are two methods the classroom teacher can use to improve students' reading comprehension strategies.

Reciprocal Teaching

Reciprocal teaching is composed of four strategies that are presented as an ongoing dialogue between the teacher and the students so that together they can interpret the meaning of text (Palinscar 1986, Palinscar and Brown 1984). With practice, the control of these strategies is gradually transferred from the teacher to the students.

The first strategy is *summarizing*. Summarizing involves paraphrasing the main idea of a paragraph. The second strategy is *question generating*, which is a form of self-testing where the reader anticipates the questions a teacher might ask on a test. Then there's *clarifying*, which is a strategy for recognizing and making clear any comprehension failures. It includes such activities as re-reading, reading ahead, asking for assistance, and using reference materials. The final strategy is *predicting*, or anticipating what the next paragraph will be about.

Initially, the teacher is responsible for demonstrating these four strategies and then takes turns using these strategies with individual students. This turn-taking is essential because students have difficulty carrying out these strategies at first.

The reading material selected for reciprocal teaching should not be so difficult that children have major decoding problems; children should make no more than two decoding errors per minute. The reading material should also be representative of the type of material children will encounter in school.

It is also imperative that teachers give students corrective feedback about how they are carrying out these strategies. The reciprocal dialogue between teacher and student, along with teaching comprehension skills in the context they will be used (while reading), combine to make reciprocal teaching successful. Figure 5.2 illustrates how teachers should present and carry out reciprocal teaching during each day's lesson.

To evaluate the success of reciprocal teaching, teachers need to use frequent and concrete measures of success. Palincsar (1986) suggests the teacher tape-record the class as it uses the reciprocal teaching strategies and then play back earlier tapes to show students how they have improved.

Another suggestion is to graph each student's performance (grades) on all assignments and tests that relate to the reading materials used in reciprocal teaching. The children can then compare these grades with previous grades made before they began using the reciprocal teaching strategies.

As in all strategy instruction, teachers should explicitly point out how students' performance has improved as a result of using the reciprocal reading strategies. These measures of success should also be adapted to other instructed strategies.

Cooperative Learning

In the typical elementary classroom, children spend up to one-half of their reading time doing independent seatwork activities (Anderson et al. 1985). Cooperative learning takes better advantage of this unsupervised time by turning it into instructionally relevant dialogue between students (Slavin 1983).

Cooperative learning occurs when four to six students of various achievement levels work together as a team, providing

75

FIGURE 5.2

RECIPROCAL TEACHING

||||||||||||||||||||||||||||||||||||||||||||||||||||||||||||||||||||||||||||||||||||||||||||||||||||||||||||||||||||

BEFORE EACH DAY'S RECIPROCAL TEACHING BEGINS:

- Teacher **reviews** the reciprocal teaching strategies with the students.

- Teacher (and students) review the **importance** of using these strategies for learning.

- Teacher (and students) review **when** to use the strategies.

- Teacher presents the title of the reading material and encourages students to discuss what they **already know** about the topic.

- Students make **predictions** about what they will learn.

- Students indicate what they would **like** to learn.

RECIPROCAL TEACHING BEGINS:

- **Teacher** is responsible for the first segment of text:

    - The teacher reads and **summarizes** what was read.

    - The teacher asks **questions** about the material.

    - The teacher leads discussion of **clarifications**.

    - The teacher invites students to elaborate and **predict** what is coming next.

- Individual students now take turns carrying out the reciprocal teaching, receiving constant reminders and feedback from the teacher.

explanations to one another about various strategies for problem solving and why certain responses are correct. Incentives for group cooperation are provided through group rewards or recognition based on the group's academic performance. Every student, however, must be held accountable for learning the new skills and cooperating in the group for cooperative learning to be effective. Cooperative learning works because: (1) students see others in various stages of mastery of the task; (2) peers provide support and assistance to one another; (3) students explain strategies to one another in their own words; and (4) it causes students to reflect on their own knowledge (Stevens, Slavin, and Farnish 1991). Cooperative learning is not a substitute for teacher-directed instruction but rather is a complementary learning activity that does not have to be led by the teacher.

An overview of the cooperative learning process is presented in Figure 5.3. Similar to reciprocal teaching, the teacher initially provides ongoing guidance, feedback, and support as students practice cooperative learning methods in their groups. Over time, however, the students begin to take on more and more responsibility and eventually carry out the cooperative learning process independently.

Many successful cooperative learning programs and materials have been developed, such as the Cooperative Integrated Reading and Composition Program (CIRC) and its corresponding materials (Stevens, Slavin, and Farnish 1991). See Figure 5.4 for an outline of this program.

Space Strategy Instruction in Mathematics

There is little consensus about the best way to teach arithmetic to elementary children (Resnick 1989). Two very different methods are currently debated. One focuses on *automaticity* in retrieval of basic number facts. This method advocates substantial drill on number facts and stresses speed as well as accuracy during instruction. The other method emphasizes *number sense* or children's need to understand the number

FIGURE 5.3

OVERVIEW OF COOPERATIVE LEARNING*

||||||||||||||||||||||||||||||||||||||||||||||||||||||||||||||||||||||||||||||||||||||||||||||||||||||||||||

STEP 1:   **Teacher-directed instruction**

Initial instruction always comes from the teacher.

STEP 2:   **Team practice**

Students work together in four-to-five-member mixed ability teams to practice the material presented by the teacher. They may complete worksheets or practice materials, discuss answers, test each other, drill one another, and so on.

STEP 3:   **Individual assignment**

Students are individually assessed on their learning of the material presented in Steps 1 and 2.

STEP 4:   **Team recognition**

Students' scores on individual assessments are averaged to form team scores. Team achievement is recognized with certificates, etc.

*Adapted from Stevens et al. 1991

FIGURE 5.4, PART 1

EXAMPLE OF A COOPERATIVE
INTEGRATED READING PROGRAM*

||||||||||||||||||||||||||||||||||||||||||||||||||||||||||||||||||||||||||||||||||||||||||||||||||||||||

STEP 1:   **Teacher-Directed Instruction**
- Students use their regular readers and are assigned to one of three reading groups based on their reading ability.
- The teacher works with students in reading groups (introduces the story and presents any new vocabulary, reviews old vocabulary, listens to children read, etc.).

STEP 2:   **Team Practice**
- When not working with the teacher in a reading group, students work together in teams of four to five members.
- Each member of a team has a partner from her/his reading group. For example, a team might consist of two partners from the top reading group and two from the low group. Team activities consist of:

> **- Partner reading**   Students first read the story silently, then orally with their partners. They take turns reading aloud, and the listener follows along and corrects errors.

> **-Story structuring**   Halfway through the story, students stop and describe the characters, location, plot, etc., and predict the ending. These descriptions are carried out again at the end of the story.

> **-Story retelling**   After reading the story, students summarize the main points with their partners.

> **-Reading words aloud**   Students practice reading a list of new and difficult words from the story. They practice with teammates until they can read them accurately.

FIGURE 5.4, PART 2

EXAMPLE OF A COOPERATIVE
INTEGRATED READING PROGRAM

||||||||||||||||||||||||||||||||||||||||||||||||||||||||||||||||||||||||||||||||||||||||||||||||||||||||||||||||||||||||

STEP 2: **Team Practice, cont.**

> **-Defining words** Students are asked to look up in a dictionary the new words from the story, paraphrase the definition, and write a sentence using each word. Teammates quiz one another over the definition.

> **-Partner checking** Students initial a student assignment form when their partners have completed each of the activities listed above.

> **-Independent reading** Students read a book of their choice for at least 20 minutes every evening. This is verified by parents' initials on forms. Students write at least one book report every two weeks (for team points). Independent reading and book reports replace all other reading homework.

STEP 3: **Individual Assessment**

After three class periods, students are given a comprehension test on the story. They are asked to write meaningful sentences for each vocabulary word and to read the word list aloud to the teacher. Students do **not** help one another with these activities.

STEP 4: **Team Recognition**

Teams that collectively averaged at least 90 percent on all activities when individually assessed are designated "Superteams" and receive certificates. Teams that average 80-89 percent are "Great Teams" and also receive certificates.

*Adapted from Stevens, Madden, Slavin, and Farnish 1987

system. Proponents of this method do believe that children need to learn their number facts, but they do not place much emphasis on drill, and even less on speed.

Research has thus far not validated one of these methods as superior to the other, nor has it shown how school drill on number facts, or even on number problems, promotes mathematical expertise (Resnick 1989). Cross-cultural research reveals that in Japan, for example, children work on only two or three mathematical problems at one time in class and spend most of their class time discussing the underlying principles related to those problems. In American classrooms, the reverse is usually the case—there is relatively little discussion, and children spend most of their time independently working on a multitude of math problems (Stiglar and Baranes 1993). The assumption in many American classrooms appears to be that with enough experience solving mathematical problems, children will eventually come to understand and appreciate underlying mathematical principles. Japanese children, however, usually demonstrate higher mathematical achievement than do American children (Stevenson et al. 1986).

One interesting aspect of children's mathematical development is that even without instruction, children will invent informal strategies of their own for solving arithmetic problems, and they usually do not rely on any one strategy, but instead develop a variety of procedures (Siegler and Shrager 1984). The following is a list of strategies that children have been observed to use spontaneously to solve addition, subtraction, and multiplication problems.

1. *Counting objects*, usually fingers, occurs when children hold up their fingers to represent the problem integers and then count all of them either silently or aloud. Another related *fingers* strategy occurs when children hold up their fingers, but solve the problem without overtly counting.

2. Children sometimes use a *counting* strategy where they count either aloud or silently, but they do not use external referents.

3. *Counting on* occurs when children start with the addend and then count out the second amount. For example, when adding 4 + 5, the child would say "4 . . . . 5, 6, 7, 8, 9."

4. *Min* is a strategy children use when they begin "counting on" with the largest integer in order to minimize the number of counts required. When adding 4 + 5, a child would begin "5 . . . 6, 7, 8, 9."

5. By age nine, when solving subtraction problems, many children either *count up* from the smaller number or *count down* from the larger, whichever requires fewer counts.

6. To multiply, children sometimes rely on *addition* to solve the problem.

7. Children often make *hatch marks* on their paper and count these marks, and sometimes base their answers on those of *related problems*.

8. *Retrieval* takes place when children recover the answer from long-term memory without using any overt strategy.

Siegler has outlined a comprehensive model of the use and development of such strategies for solving arithmetic problems (Siegler et al. 1982, 1984, 1989). According to this model, children first attempt to retrieve an answer from their long-term memory, and only when retrieval fails to provide an answer, do they revert to one of the backup strategies previously listed. Using these backup strategies does not increase the number of errors children make. In fact, children make more mathematical errors when they are not allowed to use them. Usually, children choose the fastest strategy that they can execute accurately. With increased experience in solving arithmetic problems, they tend to change their strategies. Children do not, however, substitute one strategy for another, but continue to rely on a variety of strategies for solving arithmetic problems (Siegler and Jenkins 1989). Also, experience computing (via strategies) the correct solution to individual problems increases the likelihood that individual answers will be stored in long-term memory and retrieved in the future without the need for a backup strategy.

The following are suggestions classroom teachers can use to increase children's knowledge of arithmetic facts as well as their mathematical competency and understanding.

1. *Allow children to use strategies.* Researchers warn against actively suppressing the strategies that children invent (Resnick 1989). In fact, teachers should encourage children to use the informal strategies they have developed for solving arithmetic problems. After all, these are strategies that children have invented because of their understanding of numbers and counting; they should be encouraged to use this understanding.

   Some investigators propose teaching children about the informal methods that many children develop on their own to solve arithmetic problems (Fuson and Secada 1986). The cooperative learning method described earlier for reading instruction could be revised to do this. Children in groups could describe to one another the methods they use to solve mathematical problems as well as why these methods work. As in reading, this initially requires active teacher supervision and feedback, but the teacher's role can gradually be eliminated.

2. *Teach estimation strategies:* When children's computations are incorrect, they often are outrageously inaccurate. One strategy children can be taught is to estimate the answer to a given problem before they compute the exact solution. Estimation should first be introduced by using problems that are easy for children to compute. As with other strategy

instruction, the teacher should first model estimation and then gradually let students carry out the procedures independently. Siegler (1991) proposes that other experiences with numbers, besides calculations, will help children improve their estimation abilities. For example, teachers can relate estimation with shopping. After making a purchase, we have less money than we started with. When solving a subtraction problem, the answer will also always be less; if not, then an error has been made. Teachers can demonstrate this further when children order books through the classroom book-club, pay for their lunch, and so on.

3. *Check your work:* Teachers may tell children to check their work, but often children do not understand the methods that allow them to do so or why it is important to use these methods. Teachers should not only model self-checking strategies, but should also provide students with rationales concerning *why* these strategies work (how they are related to the computations they are carrying out) and how checking improves accuracy. Increasing children's computational accuracy also increases the likelihood that correct mathematical facts will be stored in long-term memory. For example, after completing an assignment, students may check their computations by using a calculator, recomputing the problem, or engaging in a related operation (e.g., addition to check subtraction).

4. *Personalization:* Presenting mathematical examples, explanations, and problems in a format that is personal to individual students has been found to be beneficial (Anand and Ross 1987). Personalization not only increases children's interest, but also activates appropriate mental images or mental sets for understanding the material (Davis-Dorsey, Ross, and Morrison 1991). Teachers can personalize the lesson for students, and they can also instruct students in personalization. Personalization has been documented as especially beneficial

to elementary students while they are solving word problems because students often have difficulty translating mathematical word problems into the form necessary for effective computation. Personalization helps them do this. Figure 5.5 gives an example of personalization instruction.

5. *Number facts:* Throughout the day, teachers can present games and activities to promote the learning of number facts. Any activity that relates to numerals can be used to reinforce number facts. For example, a teacher may tell students that they will be receiving three handouts to complete their next assignment. The teacher can ask students how many total handouts are needed if there are 25 students in class. Or, when dividing into cooperative learning groups of five children each, the teacher can ask students to calculate how many groups will be formed. And at various points throughout the day, the teacher can ask students how many minutes until recess, lunch, the end of the day, etc.

Memorization

Throughout their elementary school career, children are faced with the task of memorizing spelling words, definitions, facts, procedures, and so on. The following elaboration, organization, and self-testing strategies help make the memorization processes easier.

Elaboration

Elaboration is a memory technique in which students create a verbal or visual association between two or more items; this association, in turn, helps them recall a related concept. For example, remembering that we reset our clocks one hour ahead in the spring and one hour behind in the fall by reciting the phrase, "spring forward, fall back," is a verbal elaborative device.

Visual elaborative strategies provide *pictorial support* of a similar nature and can be very helpful to elementary students. For example, Ehri, Deffner, and Wilce (1984) reported that students

FIGURE 5.5

AN EXAMPLE OF PERSONALIZATION INSTRUCTION

||||||||||||||||||||||||||||||||||||||||||||||||||||||||||||||||||||||||||||||||||||||||||||||||||||||||||||||

Word problem: Bill's favorite box of candy had eight pieces of candy in each of six rows. There were three layers of this candy in the box. How many pieces of candy were there in the whole box?

Teacher: How can we personalize this problem?

Students: We can relate it to someone or something we each know.

Teacher: Good. Now what, specifically, in this problem can each of us change in order to relate it to someone and something we know?

Students: We can change Bill's name to someone we know and make the candy a kind the person likes.

Teacher: Very good. Tell me, Sara, who do you know that likes candy?

Sara: My sister, Heather.

Teacher: OK. What kind of candy does Heather like the best?

Sara: Taffy.

Teacher: OK, class. How can Sara personalize this problem?

Students: She changes Bill's name to Heather and candy to taffy.

Teacher: Good. Sara, read your personalized problem for us.

Sara: Heather's favorite box of taffy had eight pieces of taffy in each of six rows. There were three layers of this taffy in the box. How many pieces of taffy were there in the whole box?

Teacher: Very good. You are ready to solve the problem. Sean, who do you know who likes candy?

learned more phonics when the letter-sound associations were each represented by a picture whose shape included the letter (e.g. letter "f" drawn as the stem of a flower). (See Figure 5.6 for other examples.) Visual methods can be used in all areas of the curriculum, not just in reading. For example, in a science lesson, teachers can present a picture of efferent neurons "exiting" (with exit signs) and afferent neurons "approaching" the central neurous system.

Although there is evidence that verbal and visual elaborations can improve young children's learning, students do not spontaneously begin to use elaborative strategies for learning until adolescence (Pressley et al. 1981). Until such time, elementary students must rely on teachers and instructional materials to provide the elaborations that will make memorization easier. They must also rely on teachers to prompt them at the time of testing or recall to use the elaborative strategies they have been taught. Research shows that while elementary students can be taught elaborative strategies, they are not likely to use these strategies later if not reminded to do so (Pressley and Levin 1980).

A specific visual strategy that has been successfully taught to students of various ages is the *keyword* method. The keyword method was originated by Atkinson and Raugh (1975) and adapted by Pressley (1977) for children's learning. The keyword method can be applied to the learning of factual information, such as the meanings for new vocabulary words or the spellings of the 50 states. This method uses a keyword mediator to facilitate remembering. The keyword is a word that either sounds similar (e.g., *pencil* for *Pennsylvania*), is spelled similarly (*transportation* for *transpiration*), or is a part of the actual word to be learned (*pepsi* for *pepsin*), and an interactive image of the word to be remembered. The keyword is then generated to aid memory. For example, to remember that *carlin* means old woman, *car* would be used as the keyword, and students would be presented with a picture of an old woman in a car (with the word *carlin* somewhere on the page). To remember that the Spanish

87

FIGURE 5.6

VISUAL ELABORATION

This example of visual elaboration shows how students learn phonics more easily when letter-sound associations are represented by a picture whose shape includes the letter.

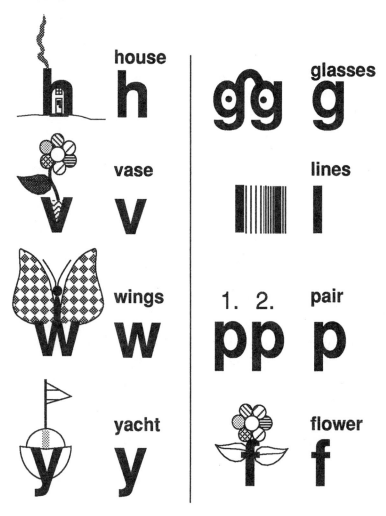

house — h h

glasses — g g

vase — v v

lines — l l

wings — w w

pair — pp p

yacht — y y

flower — f f

word *carta* means letter, a picture of a cart full of letters could be used. Levin and his colleagues have developed keyword mediators for remembering the states and their capitals. See Levin et. al (1980, 1982) for a complete description. (Also see Figure 1.2 in Chapter 1.)

Providing pictures during instruction is critical for elementary students to benefit from the keyword method. Research shows that children as young as seven years of age have benefited by instruction in the keyword method when pictorial supports are provided (Pressley et al. 1989). When using the keyword method in the classroom, the keywords selected should be words that are familiar to students and that closely represent the vocabulary words students are to learn. The less this resemblance, the less likely that the keyword will be recovered when the vocabulary word is tested via a recall test, and if the keyword is not remembered, students will also not recall the elaboration that was formed to aid their memory (Pressley et al. 1989). As with other strategy training, successful keyword instruction requires teachers to provide constructive feedback and monitoring (Pressley et al. 1989).

There are many words or expressions that do not have obvious keywords and will, therefore, not benefit from the keyword method. But for those that do, the keyword method has proven to be an invaluable strategy in learning situations.

Organization

Semantic organization is a study skill that gradually unfolds during the course of the second through fifth or sixth grades. Although young elementary students can group or categorize materials, they are rarely observed doing so in study situations unless specifically told to do so. The suggestions in Chapter 4 to promote organization in kindergarten and first grade children can be modified and used with older students as well. In addition, whenever possible, teachers should help students discover specific learning materials that can be reordered or grouped based on common attributes. For example, students

FIGURE 5.7

SELF-TESTING INSTRUCTIONS

|||||||||||||||||||||||||||||||||||||||||||||||||||||||||||||||||||||||||||||||||||||||||||||||||||||||||||||||||||||||||||||||||

Teacher: Who studied for the spelling test?

Students: *(Students raise hands.)*

Teacher: How did you know when you knew the words and could stop studying?

Students: *(Students shrug shoulders; say they don't know.)*

Teacher: How do I know when you know your spelling words?

Students: You give us a test.

Teacher: Right. How could you give yourselves a test so you would know when you knew the words well enough to stop studying?

Students: You could write the words down without looking at them. You could get your mom or dad or brother or sister or friend to give you a test.

Teacher: Good. And what should you do after you or someone else gives a test?

Students: *(Students shrug their shoulders.)*

Teacher: You should check to see if your answers are correct. If a word is not spelled correctly, you have not learned that word yet and need to study more. How will you know when you can stop studying it?

Students: *(Students don't know.)*

Teacher: You know you can stop studying when you test yourself and spell all the words correctly. By doing this, you will be **sure** you know all the spelling words and you will earn a good grade. Let me demonstrate how you can test yourself. (Teacher demonstrates, students practice, and teacher gives corrective feedback.)

can be asked to group their spelling words according to common characteristics, such as prefixes, suffixes, beginning letters, beginning sounds, and so on. When learning math facts, students can categorize according to odd and even answers, identical answers (i.e., 3 + 5 = 8, 7 + 1 = 8, 2 x 4 = 8, 10–2 = 8), and so on. For reading assignments, characters can be grouped according to similarities (e.g., age, size, importance in story). When learning states and their products, states can be organized based on common products (i.e. all states which produce corn can be listed together). Because most (if not all) learning materials can be organized in some manner, and because organizational strategies facilitate learning, elementary students will benefit each time teachers provide an organizational framework for learning and make students aware of this framework.

Self-Testing

Self-testing is a strategy in which students test themselves to determine their learning success and how much longer they need to study. Self-testing is a general strategy that can be used in all study situations for all subject areas. Teachers should instruct students in how to self-test as well as point out that self-testing gives students information about what items they need to continue studying and whether or not they can stop their studying. Figure 5.7 presents an example of instruction in self-testing techniques in dialogue form.

CONCLUSION

Because students spontaneously use more and more learning strategies from the second grade on, elementary teachers are in the perfect position to foster such development. In fact, children will not use strategies if the classroom does not support their use. Students must believe these strategies enhance performance and that strategic activity is valued. Strategy instruction alone is not a panacea for all learning difficulties children may encounter, but an environment that nourishes the use of strategies allows elementary children the opportunity to eventually learn to monitor and regulate their own learning and to master basic skills and factual information.

REFERENCES

Anand, R., and Ross, S.M. "Using Computer-Assisted Instruction to Personalize Math Learning Materials for Elementary School Children." *Journal of Educational Psychology* 79 (1987): 72–79.

Anderson, L., Brubaker, N., Alleman-Brooks, J., and Duffy, G. "A Qualitative Study of Seatwork in First Grade Classrooms." *Elementary School Journal* 86 (1985): 123–40.

Atkinson, R.C., and Raugh, M.R. "An Application of the Mnemonic Keyword Method to the Acquisition of a Russian Vocabulary." *Journal of Experimental Psychology: Human Learning and Memory* 104 (1975): 126–33.

August, D.L., Flavell, J.H., and Clift, R. "Comparison of Comprehension Monitoring of Skilled and Less Skilled Readers." *Reading Research Quarterly* 20 (1984): 39–53.

Beck, I.L., and McKeown, M. "Instructional Research in Reading: A Retrospective." In *Reading Comprehension,* edited by J. Orasanu. Hillsdale, N.J.: Erlbaum, 1986.

Daneman, M., and Carpenter, P. "Individual Differences in Working Memory and Reading." *Journal of Verbal Learning and Verbal Behavior* 19 (1980): 450–66.

Daneman, M., and Green, I. "Individual Differences in Comprehending and Producing Words in Context." *Journal of Memory and Language* 25 (1986): 1–18.

Davis-Dorsey, J., Ross, S.M., and Morrison, G.R. "The Role of Rewording and Context Personalization in the Solving of Mathematical Word Problems." *Journal of Educational Psychology* 83 (1991): 61–68.

Ehri, L. C., Deffner, N. D., and Wilce, L. S. "Pictorial Mnemonics for Phonics." *Journal of Educational Psychology* 76 (1984): 880–93.

Fuson, K.C., and Secada, W.G. "Teaching Children to Add by Counting-On with One-handed Finger Patterns." *Cognition and Instruction* 3 (1986): 229–60.

Ghatala, E.S., Levin, J.R., Pressley, M., and Goodwin, D. "A Componental Analysis of the Effects of Derived and Supplied

Strategy-Utility Information on Children's Strategy Selection." *Journal of Experimental Child Psychology* 41 (1986): 76–92.

Guttantag, R.E. "Memory and Aging: Implications for Theories of Memory Development During Childhood." *Developmental Review* 5 (1985): 56–82.

Hall, W.S. "Reading Comprehension." *American Psychologist* 44 (1989): 157–61.

Jorm, A.F., and Share, D.L. "Phonological Recoding and Reading Acquisition." *Applied Psycholinguistics* 4 (1983): 103–47.

Kee, D.W., and Bell, T.S. "The Development of Organizational Strategies in the Storage and Retrieval of Categorical Items in Free-Recall Learning." *Child Development* 52 (1981): 1163 2D–71.

Leal, L., Crays, N., and Moely, B.E. "Training Children to Use a Self-Monitoring Study Strategy in Preparing for Recall: Maintenance and Generalization Effects." *Child Development* 56 (1985): 643–53.

Lesgold, A.M., and Perfetti, C.A. *Interactive Processes in Reading.* Hillsdale, N.J.: Erlbaum, 1981.

Levin, J.R., Berry, J.K., Miller, G.E., and Bartell, N.P. "More on How (and How Not) to Remember the States and Their Capitals." *Elementary School Journal* 82 (1982): 379–88.

Levin, J.R., Shriberg, L.K., Miller, G.E., McCormick, G.B., and Levin, B.B. "The Keyword Method in the Classroom: How to Remember the States and Their Capitals." *Elementary School Journal* 80 (1980): 185–91.

Markman, E.M. "Realizing That You Don't Understand: Elementary School Children's Awareness of Inconsistencies." *Child Development* 50 (1979): 643–55.

McShane, J. *Cognitive Development: An Information-Processing Approach.* Cambridge, Mass.: Basil Blackwell, 1991.

Moely, B.E., Olson, F.A., Halwes, T.G., and Flavell, J.H. "Production Deficiency in Young Children's Clustered Recall." *Developmental Psychology* 1 (1969): 26–34.

Morais, J., Cary, L., Alegria, J., and Berelson, P. "Does Awareness of Speech as a Sequence of Phones Arise Spontaneously?" *Cognition* 7 (1979): 323–31.

Naus, M.J., Ornstein, P.A., and Kreshtool, K. "Developmental Differences in Recall and Recognition." *Journal of Experimental Child Psychology* 23 (1977): 237–51.

Nicholls, J.G. "Conceptions of Ability and Achievement Motivation: A Theory and Its Implications for Education." In *Learning and Motivation in the Classroom,* edited by S.G. Paris, G.M. Olson, and H.W. Stevenson (eds.), Hillsdale, N.J.: Erlbaum, 1983.

Olson, R.K., Kliegel, R., Davidson, B.J., and Davies, S.E. "Development of Phonetic Memory in Disabled and Normal Readers." *Journal of Experimental Child Psychology* 37 (1984): 187–206.

Ornstein, P.A., and Naus, M.J. "Rehearsal Processes in Children's Memory." In *Memory Development in Children,* edited by P. A. Ornstein (ed.), Hillsdale, N.J.: Erlbaum, 1978.

Palincsar, A.S. "Metacognitive Strategy Instruction." *Exceptional Children* 53 (1986): 118–24.

Palincsar, A.S., and Brown, A.L. "The Reciprocal Teaching of Comprehension Fostering and Comprehension Monitoring Activities." *Cognition and Instruction* 1 (1984): 117–75.

Pressley, M. "Imagery and Children's Learning: Putting the Picture in Developmental Perspective." *Review of Educational Research* 47 (1977): 586–622.

Pressley, M. "Comparing Hall (1988) with Related Research on Elaborative Mnemonics." *Journal of Educational Psychology* 83 (1991): 165–70.

Pressley, M., Goodchild, F., Fleet, J., Zajchowski, R., and Evans, D.E. "The Challenges of Classroom Strategy Instruction." *Elementary School Journal* 89 (1989): 301–42.

Pressley, M., and Levin, J.R. "Developmental Constraints Associated with Children's Use of the Keyword Method for Foreign Language Vocabulary Learning." *Journal of Experimental Child Psychology* 26 (1978): 359–73.

Pressley, M., and Levin, J.R. "The Development of Mental Imagery Retrieval." *Child Development* 51 (1980): 558–60.

Pressley, M., and Levin, J.R. "The Keyword Method and Recall of Vocabulary Words from Definitions." *Journal of Experimental Psychology: Human Learning and Memory* 7 (1981): 72–76.

Pressley, M., Samuel, J., Hershey, M.M., Bishop, S.L., and Dickinson, D. "Use of a Mnemonic Technique to Teach Young Children Foreign Language Vocabulary." *Contemporary Educational Research* 6 (1981): 110–16.

Resnick, L.B. "Developing Mathematical Knowledge." *American Psychologist* 44 (1989): 162–69.

Schneider, W. "The Role of Conceptual Knowledge and Metamemory in the Development of Multiplication Skill. *Journal of Experimental Psychology: General* 117 (1988): 258–75.

Siegler, R.S. *Children's Thinking* (2nd ed.). Englewood Cliffs, N.J.: Prentice Hall, 1991.

Siegler, R.S., and Jenkins, E. *How Children Discover New Strategies.* Hillsdale, N.J.: Erlbaum, 1989.

Siegler, R.S., and Robinson, M. "The Development of Numerical Understanding." In *Advances in Child Development and Behavior,* edited by H. Reese and L.P. Lipsitt. New York: Academic Press, 1982.

Siegler, R.S., and Shrager, J. "A Model of Strategy Choice." In *Origins of Cognitive Skills,* edited by C. Sophian. Hillsdale, N.J.: Erlbaum, 1984.

Slavin, R.E. "When Does Cooperative Learning Increase Student Achievement?" *Psychological Bulletin* 94 (1983): 429–45.

Stevens, R.J., Madden, N.A., Slavin, R.E., and Farnish, A.M. "Cooperative Integrated Reading and Composition: Two Field Experiments." *Reading Research Quarterly* 22 (1987): 433–54.

Stevens, R.J., Slavin, R.E., and Farnish, A.M. "The Effects of Cooperative Learning and Direct Instruction in Reading Comprehension Strategies on Main Idea Identification." *Journal of Educational Psychology* 83 (1991): 8–16.

Stevenson, H.W., Lee, S.Y., Stigler, J.W., Kitamura, S., Kimura, S., and Kato, T. "Achievement in Mathematics." In *Child Development and Education in Japan,* edited by H. W. Stevenson, H. Azuma, and K. Hakuta. New York: Freeman, 1986.

Stigler, J.W. and Baranes, R. "Culture and Mathematics Learning." In *Review of Research in Education,* edited by E. Rothkopf. Washington, D.C.: American Educational Research Association, (in press).

Chapter 6

MEMORY AND STUDY SKILLS IN THE MIDDLE GRADES

> *Teacher: "Gosh, Henry, you did well on the test! That was a lot to remember."*
> *Student: "It wasn't hard—I studied a special way."*
> *Teacher: "What way was that?"*
> *Student: "I followed this idea where you make a sentence with words that begin with the same letter as what you want to remember. It's easy."*
> *Teacher: "Where did you learn that?"*
> *Student: "I saw it on TV, but I can make up the sentences myself—for anything!"*
> *Teacher: "I'm impressed!"*

The middle grades (grades five or six through nine) are a critical period in the instruction of study skills for two reasons. First, middle grade students are developmentally ready to become strategic learners—their knowledge of how memory works and learning occurs is greater, they are much better able to monitor their learning efforts, and they can now adopt learning strategies without teacher prompting. In fact, they can even generate their own learning strategies. Second, the middle years represent transitional years between the elementary grades (where teachers largely control learning time, frequently monitor and evaluate student progress, and provide specific learning strategies) and high school (where teachers expect greater capacity for independent learning, where students are given responsibility for organizing study time, and where evaluations are fewer and teacher-student contact somewhat lessened). Thus, it is in the middle grades that important instruction in study skills can and must occur to bridge this gap in expectations (Adams, Carnine, and Gersten 1982). This chapter begins by describing children's strategic development during the middle grades and then presents suggestions for helping middle grade students develop both general and curriculum-related study skills.

STRATEGIC DEVELOPMENT IN THE MIDDLE GRADES

Cognitively, middle grade students are in what Jean Piaget called the *concrete operational stage;* they depend on known experiences for understanding and on physical manipulation in problem solving. As a result, middle grade students learn best through concrete demonstrations and still find pictures and visual supports helpful.

Most students are in the final steps of this dependency, and some may be beginning to make the transition into formal thought. Regardless of their status in this stage, all children in the early middle grades are logical thinkers, capable of reversing operations mentally and of noting relationships between familiar concepts.

While students should be spontaneously using such strategies as rehearsal and chunking (see Chapters 1 and 2 for descriptions of these strategies), more mature strategies involving elaboration (visual imagery, drawing associations, etc.) and rearranging material in organized and meaningful ways may not emerge without guidance and practice for the majority of students in the middle grades (Flavell 1979, Flavell and Wellman 1977).

As students become more mature, they also begin to sense which types of tasks are especially easy or difficult for them as individuals ("I hate fill-in-the-blank tests"), to determine what certain tasks require for success ("You just can't memorize the formula; you have to be able to work the problem"), and to develop a greater repertoire of strategies to use in specific instances ("First, I'll write out the formula on the top of the page; then I'll work some problems; and then I'll try to memorize the formula by repeating it to myself"). This knowledge of strategic behavior is essential to academic success.

In addition, it is critical that middle grade students begin to self-test as a way to monitor their learning. This skill should be in place by seventh or eighth grade and is evident in the study habits of successful students. Unfortunately, many middle grade students fail to test themselves for memory and comprehension and do not develop essential strategies for success, such as using practice tests, altering the length and direction of their studying as a result of these tests, and developing a sense of how well they are remembering or understanding. These behaviors correspond to the key variables of person, task, and strategy in metacognitive development identified by Flavell (1979) and described in Chapter 2.

TEACHING GENERAL LEARNING SKILLS IN THE MIDDLE GRADES

The following section examines how middle grade teachers can help their students develop two types of general learning skills: (1) listening skills and (2) preparation skills, which are skills that help students organize themselves for learning.

Listening Skills

An important prerequisite for acquiring many basic study skills, such as understanding assignments, managing time, and taking notes, is effective listening. Students spend more time in school listening than in any other single activity—about 50 percent of class time is allocated to listening to explanations, directions, and the like (Herman 1978 and Wilt 1950).

The amount of listening increases as students enter the middle grades. So does a skill that's dependent on active listening—that of note taking (Mandlebaum and Wilson 1989). As with study skills as a whole, instruction in listening will aid many low-achieving students the most because they prefer to learn by listening over reading—a characteristic of their higher achieving peers (Deshler and Shumaker 1986, Burns and Broman 1983).

The three steps involved in the act of listening (Taylor 1973, Wolvern and Coakley 1985) are hearing, attending, and assigning meaning and understanding to the message. They are clearly illustrated in the model of information processing discussed in Chapter 1. The first step, *hearing*, involves the reception of aural stimuli through the sensory receptor (the ear). The second step, *attending*, involves selective attention and the maintenance of attention (which occurs in the sensory register and short-term memory). The final step, *assigning meaning and understanding to the message*, involves using cognitive strategies to recognize and remember information, to categorize what is said, to compare new information to what is already known, and to sequence and interpret it (Mandlebaum and Wilson 1989). Assigning meaning and understanding occurs during the transference of information from short-term to long-term memory and back to short-term (now called working memory). Figure 1.1 (see Chapter 1) compares these processes.

Specific techniques to improve listening skills are summarized by Mandlebaum and Wilson (1989) in Figure 6.1. These techniques include teaching specific listening strategies, establishing lesson goals so that students understand what to listen for, ensuring that students have to act on what is heard in some way, relating listening skills to school work across the curriculum, encouraging repetition of what is heard, encouraging meaningful interpretation through questioning, demanding comprehension, using pictorial and visual cues to help students pick up auditory cues, instructing students to recognize teacher cues that indicate what information should be remembered and/or recorded, teaching self-questioning techniques to help students monitor understanding while listening, and teaching students to use visual imagery to aid retention.

The following are methods teachers can use to improve students' listening skills.

FIGURE 6.1

TECHNIQUES TO IMPROVE
LISTENING SKILLS*

||||||||||||||||||||||||||||||||||||||||||||||||||||||||||||||||||||||||||||||||||||||||||||||||||||||||||||||||||||||||||||

LISTEN FOR:

- **Numbers** that tell assigned pages to read, problems to do, length of a report, etc.
- **Key Words** —Important words that tell you to do something:
  Verbs—Read, Work, Study, Draw, Circle, Tell, Decide, Remember, Underline, Choose, Fill-in
  Directions—Left, Right, Below, Upper, Lower, Top, Bottom, Corner
- Important words are often repeated or emphasized by the teacher.
- When listening for worksheet directions, make marks.
- Picture directions (create visual images, e.g. circle the correct answer).
- Repeat directions in your own words. Summarize.
- Write down the directions on a worksheet or in an assignment book.
- **Listen before drawing conclusions.** Wait until the person has finished speaking to evaluate what you have heard.
- Ask yourself questions about what is being said. Try to answer the questions. **(*Adapted from Mandlebaum and Wilson, 1989)**

USE THE ACRONYM FACT TO REMEMBER THE ACTIVE LISTENING PROCESS:

F **ocus**	➤	Direct your attention.
A **sk**	?	Ask questions about what the teacher says.
C **onnect**	*	Connect main ideas.
T **ry to Picture**	O▸O	Make mental pictures of important ideas or make a note.

1. A common way to introduce the importance of listening skills to students is to use the Message Game, an exercise in which the teacher whispers a 20- to 25-word message to one student, who then whispers it to a classmate and so on. The last classmate to hear the message says it out loud. Then the teacher tells the original message and students discuss how and why the message changed.

2. Another way to introduce active listening instruction is to have students respond to a series of questions that require careful listening. The following are suggested in the *HM Study Skills Program* (National Association of Secondary School Principals 1986):

   - Do they have a fourth of July in France?
   - Why can't a woman living in Lexington, Kentucky, be buried west of the Mississippi?
   - A farmer in Montana had 40 sheep. In a blizzard, all but nine died. How many does he have left?
   - Is it legal for a man to marry his widow's sister?
   - Some months have 31 days. Some months have 30 days. How many have 28?
   - A plane crashed on the border between the United States and Mexico, in fact, right in the middle of the Rio Grande. In which country would the survivors be buried?

   The class discusses the answers and then tries to determine why people frequently answer these questions incorrectly and why listening errors, in general, are easily made. (Common causes of listening errors are listed in Figure 6.2.)

3. For specific examples of aiding in listening comprehension, consult *125 Ways to be a Better Student* (LinquiSystems 1989). The book stresses two basic ideas: (1) Students should learn to listen for important words, which can be used as comprehension keys; and (2) Students should try to categorize listening

FIGURE 6.2

COMMON CAUSES OF LISTENING ERRORS*

||||||||||||||||||||||||||||||||||||||||||||||||||||||||||||||||||||||||||||||||||||||||||||||||||||||||||||||||||||||||||||

- Focusing on a single word rather than on an entire question or sentence

- Jumping to a conclusion based on your expectations rather than on what's actually been said

- Not understanding or paying attention to key words

- Switching the order of words

- Not noticing verb tense or other indications of when something happened

* From HM Study Skills Program, Level V, Teacher's Guide, NASSP, 1986

material into visual reminders instead of depending simply on memory. Listening for important words can be taught through exercises that require students to listen to a series of directions and carry them out as they listen. Categorizing listening material into visual reminders can be taught by using the keyword method. (See the Writing Skills section of this chapter.)

4. Tips for following oral directions are summarized in Figure 6.1. A helpful mnemonic to remember the steps in the active listening process is the acronym FACT (Houghton Mifflin 1986):

   - **Focus**: Direct your attention.
   - **Ask**: Ask yourself questions about what the teacher is saying.
   - **Connect**: Try to connect main ideas.
   - **Try to Picture**: Make mind pictures of important ideas.

To promote generalization and transfer, students should practice these steps with actual content material from different areas of the curriculum.

Preparatory Skills

In most cases, students entering the middle grades must cope with greater organizational demands than before: changing classes, using a locker, keeping notebooks and folders for each class, remembering assignments and homework given by multiple teachers—all without the teacher direction they were given in the elementary grades. These can be overwhelming tasks for young adolescents. The following are suggestions students can try to help organize their preparation for learning.

1. Students can use the PREPARE strategy, which was initially developed to help younger students make sure they are ready for class (Ellis and Lenz 1987). The prepare strategy consists of:

- **P**lan locker visits: "When may I go to my locker?"
- **R**eflect on what you need to get: "What books, materials, and homework do I need?"
- **E**rase personal needs: Put aside personal problems before entering class. "Do I need to use the restroom?"
- **P**sych yourself up for class: Pause for an attitude check. Set a goal for the class; think of positive points; tell yourself you can do it.
- **A**sk where the class is going: "What have we been doing? What's happening next?
- **R**eview notes and study guides: "What did we do in the last class? How will that fit into what we do today?"
- **E**xplore the meaning of the class introduction: "What should I know from this class?"

2. Students can use general mnemonics to help them remember important materials and assignments.

3. Because middle grade students respond well to concrete imagery, *personification* (as described in Chapter 5) is a technique that also works well. Personification refers to a figure of speech in which lifeless qualities become human ones. For example, if a student wanted to remember to read his history book, he might conjure up an image of the book as a familiar historical figure (such as George Washington) who is walking along side him or perched on the table where he usually does homework. If a student wants to remember to check an assignment book, a friend's face could be pictured on the notebook. Thoughts of the friend will then trigger an association to the notebook.

4. Because students begin to tackle larger independent assignments and have more material to study for individual tests in the middle grades, these grades are a good time to help students develop a *personal study system*. Study systems may be most effective when characterized by a problem-solving

approach. Teachers should emphasize six important steps for students (Haburton 1981) that can be remembered as the acronym SOLVER.

- Identify major study problems and prioritize them.
- Determine the goal or outcome to be accomplished.
- Examine and make a list of the factors that contribute to the solution.
- Visualize and generate corrective strategies to solve the problem.
- Evaluate the study plan.
- Revise if necessary.

5. To develop time-management skills, teachers should introduce students to schedules, assignment books, and other organizational devices.

Schedules may be organized by the semester, month, week, or even hour. Needs in this area vary. Whatever the format, however, Gartland (1989) suggests that students contract with peers, parents, or teachers for successful adherence to schedules.

As far as assignment books go, some students may prefer a small spiral bound notebook; others may like a calendar; still others may favor dated assignment sheets attached to each notebook. The style of the assignment book is not particularly important. The book should, however, be readily accessible and easy to record the following information in: a list of courses; the date of each assignment; assignment descriptions, including important page numbers and directions; and notation marks for completed assignments. In the early middle grades, teachers should model good assignment recording—and even tell students what to record. From time to time, students can trade assignment books and check each other's recording for accuracy. See Figure 6.3 for an example of an Assignment-Book Swap worksheet.

FIGURE 6.3

ASSIGNMENT BOOK SWAP*

||||||||||||||||||||||||||||||||||||||||||||||||||||||||||||||||||||||||||||||||||||||||||||||||||||||||||||||||

Trade assignment books with another student. Use the questions below to check each other's book.

Student: _____

Reviewer: _____

	YES	NO
• Are the day and date at the top?	——	——
• Does each subject have enough room next to it to write the assignment?	——	——
• Is there enough space at the bottom of the page to write other notes?	——	——
• Is "none" written if there was no homework in a subject?	——	——
• Did the student number the homework in order from hardest to easiest?	——	——
• Did the student check off assignments that were finished?	——	——

*Adapted from Linqui System, *125 Ways to Be a Better Student,* 1987.

Organizing study materials is also important. Teachers should encourage students to acquire the following habits:

- Keep class notes in a notebook rather than on loose leaf paper.
- Match notebooks and textbooks by color or a coding system.
- Put complete identification on all materials.
- Keep returned papers and file those for each class together.
- Organize locker or desk.

To promote transfer, these habits must be practiced and reinforced through the year and across the curriculum. Once acquired, such organizational habits carry over to high school and are evident in the practices of successful college students.

ENCOURAGING STRATEGY USE IN MIDDLE GRADE CURRICULA

The following section examines ways middle grade teachers can help their students develop learning strategies within curricular content.

Study Skills in Language Arts

During the middle grades, students are asked to deepen comprehension skills, become more skillful writers, gain mastery of grammar and punctuation, increase vocabulary, and transfer these skills to classes other than "Reading." This section discusses techniques that aid students' comprehension, help students organize and proofread, increase students' ability to retain and use grammatical and spelling rules, and help students remember vocabulary words.

Reading Comprehension

In the classroom, teachers can help students develop reading comprehension skills through questions, activities, and evaluations. Methods that have proven effective include *SQ3R* (Survey, Question, Read, Recite, Review) first introduced by Robinson (Thomson and Robinson 1972) and *PQ4R* (Preview, Question, Read, Reflect, Recite, Review). Both force students (through a series of steps) to process reading at deeper levels (Adams, Carnine, and Gersten 1982; Doctorow, Wittrock, and Marks 1978; and Hamilton 1985).

These methods conform closely to our knowledge of effective information processing as discussed in Chapter 1. By surveying and previewing material, students are able to direct selective attention effectively. By anticipating questions to be answered by the text, students establish expectations that also facilitate selective attention and ensure important information enters short-term memory. The read, reflect, recite sequence ensures the likelihood of information being understood in meaningful ways and thereby entering long-term memory. Paraphrasing information read or heard (putting it into your own words) is an excellent method for testing comprehension.

When teachers present material to their classes, they often move through these steps for students. They preview material, suggest what information students should look for, question students after reading, and present a review. The SQ3R method and other similar techniques teach students to do for themselves the things a teacher would do to facilitate comprehension and retention.

The *multipass method* (Schumaker et al. 1982) is another simple strategy for helping students understand and retain what they are reading. It includes three basic steps: (1) Survey; (2) Go back and find key information; (3) Go back and study key information. A student reading a math assignment would survey the assignment to get a general idea of the content; go back and identify key information such as formulas, definitions, or explanations of procedures or theory, and example problems; then go back and study these key pieces of information until understood. This understanding could best be assessed by the student by means of a self-test, which might constitute a fourth step. Because the multipass system is a simpler system with fewer steps, it is more likely to be used and carried out efficiently by students. This may be a system that teachers introduce before more complicated ones such as SQ3R.

Writing

In language arts, middle grade students also work to develop their writing skills: to become more organized writers and to learn to master grammar, punctuation, and spelling.

1. Many of the rules and concepts of grammar are much more easily retained through the use of rhymes and imagery. Hasentab (1988) suggests the following poem for remembering the parts of speech.

PARTS OF SPEECH
Would you rather be at the beach
Or would you like to learn the parts of speech?
Nouns are needed to make a sentence sing;
You know they're a person, place, or thing.
Every sentence has a verb;
Better use it or you're a nerd.
Adjectives bring the sentence to life;
Don't be afraid to describe your wife.
The wee little words that you also need
Are prepositions, conjunctions, not chicken feed.
Pronouns are used to replace a noun.
At the beginning of a sentence interjections are found.
"-Ly" is at the end of a word;
How, when, and where describes an adverb.
Now you can sing the parts of speech.
Your goals in life are now within reach!

2. The *keyword method* can be helpful in learning new vocabulary words and definitions. This method relies on associating a known word with an unknown word and is frequently used when learning foreign language vocabulary. It works well with most words, however (Mastropieri 1988). For

109

example, to remember the new word *gulch,* a keyword might be *sea gull.* A visual image of a sea gull flying in a canyon could remind the student that a gulch is a canyon. Such associations are best retained when the images are bizarre or vivid. To accomplish this, keep four concepts in mind (Lorayne and Lucas 1974):

> *Substitution:* Picture one item instead of another, as in the sea gull for the gulch.
> *Out of Proportion:* Try to see the items larger than life.
> *Exaggeration:* Make your images as wild as possible.
> *Action:* Try to put action in your image to aid memory.

It takes imagination to form silly, ridiculous pictures. Children, particularly those in the middle grades, will enjoy this as their concrete thinking mode finds such images especially funny. These techniques help form "links" between new and old information.

3. *Linking systems* or *chain mnemonics* are helpful in learning sequential material. Here, the student connects the first item with the second, the second with the third, and so on. This method works well when remembering steps in a problem or procedure. For example, when learning how to construct an essay, students must remember that the key elements are introduction, body or story of the essay, and summary or conclusion. A mnemonic that uses the link method might be the sentence: "Introducing the story of some Mary." In this sentence, "introducing" represents introduction, "the story" represents the body or story of the essay, and "of some Mary" represents the summary.

4. Another proofing strategy, known as *WRITER,* (Ellis and Lenz 1987) includes six steps:

  • **W**rite on every other line initially.
  • **R**ead your paper for meaning. Make sure each sentence

110

makes a point or offers support to the main theme.

- Interrogate yourself by using a second strategy called COPS to check *capitalization, overall appearance, punctuation,* and *spelling.*
- Take the paper to someone to proofread for both meaning and grammar.
- Execute a final copy. Make it neat.
- Reread your paper a final time.

This type of self-questioning aids in the development of monitoring skills and may further metacognitive awareness.

5. *Means-end analysis* requires that a problem or task be divided into a number of subproblems or subtasks so that a means of solving each aspect of the problem can be more easily deduced. For example, a research paper or project might be broken down into the following tasks: select a topic, locate sources of information, read and organize your information, make an outline (see Chapter 7), create an introductory sentence, summarize information in essay format, write summary/conclusion, and look for and examine errors. Teachers often move their students through a similar series of steps—assigning subtasks and deadline dates for each part, and even providing feedback along the way. However, teachers may not make students aware of the process or engage them in monitoring themselves. Students should become part of the means-end analysis (perhaps through small group interaction that the teacher later summarizes for the whole class) and be encouraged to monitor and evaluate their work through progress sheets. Teachers can use self-monitoring charts across the curriculum to motivate students and to help them gauge their learning. Remember that self-monitoring strategies are not learning strategies in themselves, but strategies to evaluate learning. Successful monitoring requires that students be able to perform the task. Students could monitor correct practices of repeated writing

111

of spelling words, for example. The repeated writing is a strategy for learning; the monitoring evaluates its effectiveness (Reid and Harris 1989). Teachers can record performance through a variety of graphs, charts, or checklists. "Spelling pencils" (Reid and Harris 1989) or colorful bar graphs may be especially reinforcing to younger students. (See Figure 6.4.)

Study Skills in Mathematics

By the middle grades, students should have mastered basic math facts and operations. For students who have not, exercises described in Chapter 4 are still appropriate. For example, putting math facts to rhythm or music capitalizes on the ease we generally experience in remembering jingles and song lyrics. Making rote tasks meaningful is also helpful. The following example helps students to see the relationship between the five and 10 times tables.

Teacher: You all know the five times table. Let's review: $1 \times 5 = 5$, $2 \times 5 = 10$, $3 \times 5 = 15$, $4 \times 5 = 20$, $5 \times 5 = 25$ (etc.).
Students: (Students complete the table.)
Teacher: Now, let's think about the 10 times tables. How many fives make 10?
Students: Two.
Teacher: So, 10 is 5×2, right? Then it is double five. Let's look at the ten's table: $1 \times 10 = 10$, $2 \times 10 = 20$, $3 \times 10 = 30$, $4 \times 10 = 40$, $5 \times 10 = 50$ (Teacher points to the rest on a chart). Do you see a relationship?
Students: Every ten's table answer is twice the fives table's answer.
Teacher: Yes! Is that true for all tables where one number is double another?

Solving word problems and even introducing basic algebraic equations becomes more central to math instruction in the middle grades. There are many problem solving strategies students can apply to mathematics. One general strategy that works well is *IDEAL* (Bransford et al. 1986). Here's how a

FIGURE 6.4

SPELLING PENCILS

For young children, "spelling pencils" are a good way to reinforce learning by testing. Students of all ages can record their performance through a variety of graphs, charts, or checklists.

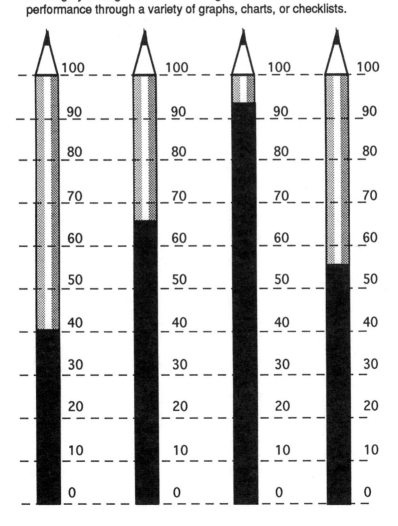

student would apply IDEAL to compute the mean cost of the items purchased at the following prices: $40.74, $39.45, $38.57, $39.05, $38.86, and $39.25.

- **Identify the problem.** Find the mean cost of this list.
- **Define the problem more precisely.** Calculate the mean of this list of numbers.
- **Explore possible solutions.** The standard method of finding the average is to divide the sum of the list by the number of items in the list.
- **Act on the solution.** Calculate the answer by using the above solution (Answer: $39.32).
- **Look at the results of the solution.** Thirty-nine point thirty-two is in the "ball park" with the other numbers on the list—this is a good solution.

Step five illustrates how important estimation is as a tool in self-testing and in increasing students' thoughtfulness about their learning. Many times in our lives we must guess about how something might turn out of we proceed a certain way. To make those guesses more accurate, students must learn to look carefully at the original problem to predict the answer. Students would eliminate many errors if they used routine estimation procedures. This skill will only generalize to other subjects, however, if students receive practice in estimation in the classroom and understand how it can help them avoid errors.

Encouraging students to verbalize problems and to "talk the problem through" is especially applicable to solving word problems. For example, a student is given the problem below:

An oil storage tank, which is in the shape of a cylinder is 4 meters high and has a 6-meter diameter. Find the volume of the oil storage tank.

The student could " talk it through" in this way:

"Let's see, I need to find the volume of this cylinder. I know that the volume of the cylinder equals pi r squared h when r equals the radius, and h is the height. The diameter of this cylinder is 6 meters, so the radius is half of the diameter, 6, which equals 3. Three squared equals 9. The height of the cylinder is 4 meters. Pi is 3.14. Now, I have to put those values into the equation pi r squared h. Hmm, I see the equation is 3.14 times 9 (the radius squared) times 4 (the value of the height). All right! Now, I can quickly calculate the answer—113.04 cubic meters.

Middle grade students should be encouraged to draw pictures or make notes as they "talk through" a problem because visualization and iconic representations are important at this developmental stage. Mnemonic tools are also helpful in memorizing important values such as pi. The value 3.14 might be retained by imagining *three* people cutting *one* pie into *four* pieces. Students might also picture themselves right before the bell rings to end the school day—3:14 p.m.

Many students have difficulty with such word problems. *SQRQCQ* (Fay 1965) is a strategy to aid students in reading mathematics word problems. The student:

- **S**urveys the problem.
- **D**ecides what question is being asked.
- **R**eads for details.
- **Q**uestions what operations should be used.
- **C**omputes the operations.
- **Q**uestions whether the answer is logical.

Again, note that this system stresses estimation and self-checking in students, skills that are essential for success, confidence, and accuracy in mathematics.

Study Skills in Social Studies and Science

Many of the techniques discussed previously are helpful to students when solving problems or preparing reports in the areas of science and social studies. In addition to these tasks, students may face the necessity of memorizing sets of facts and other important information. This is best done by placing the new facts and concepts in a meaningful context. To enhance retention and understanding, new information should be related to current knowledge. This is especially true for middle grade students who understand concepts in terms of their own experience and concrete examples.

The middle grades may be a good time to introduce *concept mapping* as both a means of understanding new concepts and related facts and as a method of note taking. Concept mapping (Collette and Chiapetta 1989) allows students to see a visual representation of the relationship between ideas. Each idea or key concept is placed in an oval. Then linking words are written on lines that connect the key concepts. Broad, general concepts appear at the top of the map, and specific examples of those concepts are at the bottom, producing a hierarchical effect.

When introducing concept mapping to students, the teacher should initially provide the framework and allow them to fill it in as the lesson proceeds. Students can check their completed maps through learning partners, cooperative learning groups (see Chapter 5), or whole class discussion. Eventually, students should create their own frameworks, which may differ slightly from student to student because they reflect individual processing.

Comparative organizers, devices in which something unknown is linked to something known, are also excellent ways to retain new concepts and facts. Collette and Chiapetta (1989) suggest that students might remember the parts of the living cell by comparing the function of each part of the cell to its counterpart in a jail cell.

Function	Jail Structure	Living Structure
outer structure	cell walls	cell wall
control center	prisoner	nucleus
environment	air	cytoplasm
communication	prisoner's voice	endoplasmic reticulum

116

energy	light bulb	mitochondria
food source	hole in door	vacuole
waste removal	plumbing	vacuole

When it comes to encoding new vocabulary in science or social studies, the *keyword method* (discussed earlier in this chapter and also in Chapter 5) can be very effective. For example, to remember what the term "sedimentary" means, tell students to think of a common term that sounds similar, such as *cement*. Cement is made up of small rocks glued together. Sedimentary rock is made up of sediments (small rocks) that are pressed (glued) together.

Following is another example.

Teacher: "I have a hard time remembering the difference between latitude and longitude. Do you? How have you tried to remember?"
Student: "Say the definition over and over."
Teacher: "That's usually a good way, but when things are really similar, it's hard to remember them. Who can show me which lines represent longitude on the map?"
Student: (points to a longitude line on the map.)
Teacher: "So, the north-south lines represent longitude. They're the long ones? You could remember the difference that way. Can you think of any other ways? Sometimes it's easier to think of something that makes sense about what you want to remember instead of just saying the definition over and over again."

The *five Ws* is a questioning technique that can help students learn historical and scientific facts within a related context. To use this technique, students ask the following questions about a specific situation:

- **Who** was involved?
- **What** happened?
- **When** did it happen?
- **Where** did it happen?
- **Why** did it happen and/or why is it significant?

Deshler and Shumaker (1986) use the following paragraph as an example:

"Michael Faraday, English physicist, reported in 1832 that when electric current is passed through a molten salt or a salt solution so as to decompose it into elementary substances, "The chemical action of the current of electricity is in direct proportion to the absolute quantity of electricity which passes."

Using the five Ws technique, students would produce the following:

Who?: Michael Faraday
What?: Electricity and chemical action are directly proportional
When: 1832
Where?: England
Why significant?: His work suggested that the electric nature of the atom involved discrete particles of electricity (which led to discovery of the electron).

A strategy that can be used for memorization is *first letter mnemonics*. To remember the Great Lakes, students might remember the word HOMES: (*Huron, Ontario, Michigan, Erie, and Superior*). To memorize the Great Lakes in their correct geographical order, students could employ the saying, "*She made Henry eat onions*" (Superior, Michigan, Huron, Erie, and Ontario). Teachers will need to provide such mnemonics because it is doubtful that middle grade students will develop their own spontaneously.

Imagery, as was mentioned earlier, is an excellent strategy to use with students in Piaget's concrete operational stage. When using this strategy, the student conjures up in his or her mind pictures or images to aid retention of material. To remember that the capital of Arkansas is Little Rock, have students visualize an *ark* that uses a *can* as a resting place on which to *saw* a *little rock*. To remember that the capital of Maine is Augusta, have them

118

picture a horse standing with *a* powerful *gust of* wind blowing its *mane*. Allowing students to actually draw the pictures may enhance the strategy's effectiveness. At this age, teachers will have to provide imagery for students; in most cases, they will not generate it spontaneously. (See Figure 1.2 in Chapter 1.)

The *loci method* uses "location" to help students remember long lists of persons, places, or things. Suppose students were asked to memorize the first 16 Presidents of the United States in order. Students could visualize a room in their home. The student begins with the first piece of furniture to the left and places George Washington there (e.g., sitting on a chair), then moves to the next adjoining location for John Adams (e.g., standing near the floor lamp) and places the third and following presidents accordingly. The familiarity with the order of the room is important to place names or objects in correct order. Instead of locating persons, places, or things near furnishings in a room a home, students could place them in front of the houses on one's street or on equipment located on the school playground.

Students in the middle grades should already be chunking small bits of information as they memorize. Chunking is also an efficient strategy that can be used to memorize long lists of items. For example, students can memorize the names of the original 13 colonies by rehearsing three groups of four colonies, with Georgia standing alone at the end.

CONCLUSION

Teachers should not only train students to be proficient in specific subject matter or problem-solving techniques, but also in general metacognitive processes. Moely et al. (1986) found that teachers seldom made suggestions regarding metamemory (knowledge of memory processes, strategies, and other factors that affect memory) and rarely provided explicit instructions, demonstrations, or feedback about the memory strategies they did suggest. This is an important finding because results from laboratory memory training studies indicate that children require this type of intensive training in order to produce lasting, transferable strategy use (Black and Rollins 1982; Leal, Cray, and Moely 1985; and Pressley, Borkowski, and O'Sullivan 1984). Teachers will not be successful in promoting strategic behavior in their students if they omit the key features of successful strategy training. Students are especially able to profit from such training in the middle grades.

REFERENCES

Adams, A, Carnine, D. and Gersten, R. "Instructional Strategies for Studying Content Area Texts in the Intermediate Grades." *Reading Research Quarterly* 18 (1982): 27–53.

Black, M.M., and Rollins, H.A., Jr. "The Effects of Instructional Variables on Young Children's Organization and Free Recall." *Journal of Experimental Child Psychology* 33 (1982): 1–19.

Bransford, J., Sherwood, R., Vye, N., and Rieser, J. "Teaching Thinking and Problem Solving." *American Psychologist* (October, 1986): 1078–89.

Brown, A.L. and Campione, J.C. "Training Strategic Studytime Apportionment in Educable Retarded Children." *Intelligence* 1 (1977): 94–107.

Burns, P.C., and Broman, B.L. *The Language Arts in Childhood Education* (5th edition). Boston: Houghton Mifflin, 1983.

Collette, A.T., and Chiapetta, E.L. *Science Instruction in the Middle and Secondary Schools.* Columbus, Ohio: Merrill Publishing Company, 1989.

Deshler, D.D., and Shumaker, J.B. "Learning Strategies: An Instructional Alternative for Low Achieving Adolescents." *Exceptional Children* 52 no. 6 (1986): 583–85.

Devine, T.G. "Listening: What Do We Know After 50 Years of Research and Theorizing?" *Journal of Reading* 21 (1978): 296–304.

Doctorow, M., Wittrock, M.C., and Marks, C. "Generative Processes in Reading Comprehension." *Journal of Educational Research* 70 (1978): 109–18.

Ellis, E.S., and Lenz, Keith B. "A Component Analysis of Effective Learning Strategies." *Learning Disabilities Focus* 2 no. 2 (1987): 94–107.

Fay, L. "Reading Study Skills: Math and Science." *Reading and Inquiry*, edited by J.A. Figurel. Newark, Del.: International Reading Association, 1965.

Flavell, J.H. "Developmental Studies of Mediated Memory." In *Advances in Child Development and Behavior*, edited by H.W. Reese and L.P. Lipsitt. New York: Academic Press, 1970.

Flavell, J.H. "Metacognition and Cognitive Monitoring." *American Psychologist* 34 (1979): 906–11.

Flavell, J.H., and Wellman, H.M. "Metamemory." In *Perspectives on the Development of Memory and Cognition*, edited by R.V. Kail and J.W. Hagen. Hillsdale, N.J.: Laurence Erlbaum Associates, 1977.

Gartland, D. "Study Skills Instruction for Students with Learning Disabilities." *Learning Disabilities Forum* 15 no.1 (Fall, 1989): 11–15.

Haburton, E.C. *Study Skills for College.* Cambridge, Mass.: Winthrop, 1981.

Hallahan, D.P., Lloyd, J.W., Kauffman, J.M., and Loper, A.B. "Academic Problems." In *The Practice of Child Therapy*, edited by R.J. Morris and T.R. Kratochwill. New York: Pergamon Press, 1983.

Hamilton, B.J. "Recent Research on Visual Mnemonics. Historical Roots and Educational Fruits." *Review of Educational Research* 55 (1985): 47–86.

Hasentab, J.K. *Patterns for IDEAS.* Performance Learning Systems, Inc., Winter, 1988.

Herman, W.L. "The Use of Language Arts in Social Studies Lessons." *American Education Review Journal* 4 (1978): 296–304.

Leal, L., Crays, N., and Moely, B.E. "Training Children to Use a Self-Monitoring Study Strategy in Preparation for Recall: Maintenance and Generalization Effects." *Child Development* 56 (1985): 643–53.

LinquiSystems. *125 Ways to Be a Better Student.* East Moline, IL: LinquiSystems Inc., 1989.

Lorayne, H. and Lucas, J. *The Memory Book.* New York: Stein and Day, 1974.

Mandlebaum, L.H. and Wilson, R. "Teaching Listening Skills" *L.D. Forum* 15 no. 1 (Fall, 1989): 7–9.

Marshak, D. *HM Study Skills Program (Level II)* Reston, Vir.: The National Association of Secondary School Principals, 1986.

Mastropieri, M. "Using the Keyword Method." *Teaching Exceptional Children* 20 no. 2 (1988): 4–8.

Moely, B.E., Hart, S.S., Santulli, K., Leal, L., Johnson, T., Rao, N., and Burney, L. "How Do Teachers Teach Memory Skills?" *Educational Psychologist* 21 (1986): 55–71.

National Association of Secondary School Principles. *HM Study Skills Program (Level II)*. Reston, Vir.: National Association of Secondary School Principles, 1986.

Palinscar, A.S., and Brown, A.L. "Reciprocal Teaching of Comprehension-Fostering and Monitoring Activities." *Cognition and Instruction* 1 (1984): 117–75.

Pressley, M., Borkowski, J.G., and O'Sullivan, J.T. "Memory Strategy Instruction is Made of This: Metamemory and Durable Strategy Use." *Educational Psychologist* 19 (1984): 94–107.

Reid, R. and Harris, K.R. "Self-Monitoring of Performance." *Learning Disabilities Forum* 15 no. 1(Fall, 1989): 39–43.

Schumaker, J.B., Deshler, D.D., Alley, G.R., and Denton, P.H. "Multipass: A Learning Strategy for Improving Reading Comprehension." *Learning Disabilities Quarterly* 5 no. 3 (1982): 295–304.

Taylor, S. *Listening: What Research Says to the Teacher*. Washington D.C.: National Education Association, 1973.

Thomson, E.L., and Robinson, H.A. *Improving Reading in Every Class: A Sourcebook for Teachers*. Boston: Allyn and Bacon, 1972.

Wilt, M.E. "A Study of Teachers Awareness of Listening as a Factor in Elementary Education." *Journal of Educational Research* 43 (1950): 626–36.

Wolvern, A.D. and Coakley, C.G. *Listening* (2nd edition). Dubuque, Iowa: William C. Brown, 1985.

Chapter 7

MEMORY AND STUDY SKILLS AT THE SECONDARY LEVEL

Imagine that prior to graduation from high school, each student was required to demonstrate an effective note-taking system, explain what he or she does to improve comprehension when reading difficult material, exhibit a study routine for different types of tests, and display a repertoire of personally relevant mnemonic devices. Who could imagine that such a student could not succeed in college?

Students at the secondary level have specific study-skill needs. The amount of independent work required of them is greater; the level of reading difficulty increases throughout the curriculum; greater demands are made on memory; and testing takes a more serious turn. This chapter discusses systems designed to aid the studying and memory skills necessary to meet these requirements, including aids for enhancing note taking, reading comprehension, and test preparation.

NOTE TAKING

Beginning at around the seventh grade, teachers increasingly rely on the lecture method to teach content (Risch and Kiewra 1990). One of the most frequently preferred study strategies for learning lecture material is note taking (Annis and Davis 1982). This section reviews the functions that note taking serves, describes possible sources of individual differences, and makes suggestions teachers can use to improve students' abilities to take and review notes.

Functions of Note Taking

Many students learn from lectures by recording lecture notes and by later reviewing those notes prior to an examination. DiVesta and Gray (1972) found that note taking does serve both an *encoding* and a *storage* function and that both of these functions facilitate learning from lectures.

Encoding

The *encoding function* relates to the actual recording of notes and how note taking enhances how students organize and process lecture information (DiVesta and Gray 1972). Researchers have investigated the encoding effects of note taking by comparing the recall performance of note takers with that of students who listen to the same lecture but do not take notes. In a review of this research literature, Ladas (1980) concluded that the experimental evidence strongly favors the encoding or learning function of note taking. For example, Bretzing, Kulhavy, and Caterino (1987) compared the multiple-choice exam performance of seventh grade students who took notes during the related lecture to those who did not. Even though note takers were *not* allowed to review their notes prior to the exam, their performance was better than the performance of those who did not take notes. Researchers have found, however, that note taking interferes with learning when the presentation rate of the lecture is fast and when the information presented is so dense that note taking competes with attentional resources needed to process the lecture (Cook and Mayer 1983).

Storage

As previously cited, taking notes aids recall. But note taking alone does not ensure recall. Some researchers feel that the main value of note taking is not the act of actually recording notes but rather the *storage function* that note taking provides for reviewing lecture content later. In his review of 22 studies, Kiewra (1985) concluded that students who review notes usually

124

achieve more than students who take notes but do not review them. Other researchers have reported that it is additionally beneficial if students review their notes *just prior* to the exam (e.g., Estes 1976). Some students, however, fail to review their notes at all (Norton 1981), which led Palkovitz and Lore (1980) to conclude that students often err on test items not because their notes are inaccurate or incomplete but because they have failed to review or study their notes adequately.

Individual Differences in Note Taking

To benefit from the storage function of note taking, however, students must have adequate notes to study (Kiewra and Fletcher 1984). Research shows that reviewing notes that are more complete yields higher achievement (Collingwood and Hughes 1978). This is important research because students often have been found to be limited in both the amount and the completeness of the notes they record. These inadequacies are not limited to beginning note takers; even college students have been found to be incomplete note takers. For example, in one study Kiewra and Frank (1988) found that college students who took notes from a videotaped lecture recorded only 24 percent of the important ideas in the lecture. Why are students at both high school and college levels poor note takers? Reasons vary, as the following information on individual note-taking differences indicates.

Information-Processing Limitations

Castallo (1976) defined note taking as a two-step process: (1) students must listen for important information, and (2) they must write down this information in an organized manner. There are, therefore, heavy information-processing demands placed on students to simultaneously listen to the lecture, process the information presented, decide what to transcribe, and actually take notes during a lecture. For this reason, some researchers recommend that students should *not* attempt to relate lecture information to previous knowledge *while* taking notes.

125

(This can be accomplished, however, while reviewing notes when students do not have to divide their attention among so many tasks.) Attempts at elaboration during note taking are difficult and often debilitating because they take up limited information-processing space that is being used to process the lecture material.

A slow writing or spelling speed compounds the processing demands for some students (Ladas 1980) and explains the tremendous difficulty many learning disabled students have in taking notes. Writing down important ideas from the lecture interferes with their mental processing and recording of subsequent lecture content.

Academic Ability

Research shows that poor learners often use less effective processing strategies, and strategies used for note taking are no exception. Einstein et al. (1985) studied note taking with successful (grade point average = 3.12) and less successful (grade point average = 1.93) college students. Einstein et al. reported no differences based on grade point average in both the amount of effort exerted during note taking and in the recall of the less important propositions from the lecture. Both groups of students also benefited equally from reviewing their notes prior to testing, and both were similar in their note-taking styles. Two main differences however, were that successful students recalled more of the most important propositions from the lecture, and they also recorded more of these high importance propositions in their notes than did less successful students. Other researchers also have reported that some students have difficulty differentiating important from unimportant information while taking notes during lectures (Palmaiter and Bennett 1974).

Lack of Instruction

Another reason many students are poor note takers is that they have not been taught effective note-taking strategies (Palmaiter and Bennett 1974; Saski, Swicegood, and Carter

1983; Sheinker and Sheinker 1982). A lack of effective strategies interferes with both the encoding and storage function of note taking.

Techniques for Improving Note-Taking Skills

This section presents techniques the classroom teacher can use to help students take adequate lecture notes.

Skeletal Notes

Skeletal notes provide students with a framework for note taking. They are basic outlines of the lecture content with blank spaces for students to record details from the lecture. Teachers must provide students with the skeletal notes before the lecture begins. Skeletal notes can consist of headings, subheadings, key words or phrases, questions, and so on. The main features of skeletal notes are that they organize the lecture content for students as well as point out important lecture information. The amount of blank space provided with skeletal notes is critical because students seem to assume that it implies the amount of information they are to record (Hartley 1976). Students who use skeletal notes often score higher on tests of lecture content than do students who do not use skeletal notes but record their own personal notes from the lecture (Kiewra 1985).

Instructor's Notes

Instead of skeletal notes, some teachers may prefer to provide students with a complete set of instructor's notes that detail all essential points made during the lecture and do not require any encoding by students. Although instructor's notes are usually more complete than the notes students record for themselves, many researchers warn against their use because they may encourage students to memorize and repeat information without understanding. Instructor's notes, likewise, may cause some students not to process or encode the information provided during the actual lecture because they feel they can rely on and "study" the instructor's notes at a later time. Kiewra and Frank

(1988) found that providing detailed instructor's notes produced higher recall of lecture material on a delayed test after students were allowed to review the notes, but not on an immediate test when students were not permitted to review the notes.

Other researchers report that students who review instructor's notes as well as their own personal notes achieve the best, but that students usually recall proportionally more of their own notes than the instructor's notes (Annis and Davis 1975). This suggests that students should be required to take their own personal notes or use skeletal notes during the lecture, and that teachers interested in providing instructor's notes should hand them out later, just before students review for an upcoming exam. This method allows students to fill in any missing information in their personal notes by using the instructor's notes.

Note-Taking Cues

Most teachers provide students with cues for what information is critical and needs to be recorded in their notes, and that's helpful. However, many students still require instruction in how to determine such cues. For example, teachers need to point out that information written on the board during a lecture is one cue for note taking. Teachers must also point out that information written on the board is usually not the only information students need to record during a lecture.

In addition, teachers should remind students that certain words or phrases are important note-taking cues. This includes "First . . . ," "The reason for . . . ," "There are three causes . . . ," "An important finding was . . . ," and so on. Other cues include repeated phrases or pauses by the lecturer.

The class as a whole (or students in groups) might find it beneficial to work together to produce a list of cues to use while note taking.

Transparencies

Researchers have found that material displayed on

prepared overhead transparencies and on slides usually presents information that is too complex to be recorded or drawn in students' notes (Hartley and Cameron 1967, Maddox and Laughran 1977, McAndrew 1983). Because students must listen and process what the teacher is saying *and* process the visual information on the transparency, this can lead to an information-processing overload, and thus students don't record all the critical information they should in their notes. When using transparencies or slides, teachers should prepare for a possible information-processing overload by previewing the material and perhaps providing students with a handout (or skeletal notes) of information to be presented.

Teachers can, however, use transparencies to model how to record notes. While working at the overhead projector with a blank transparency, the teacher can record notes while someone else is lecturing. (A videotaped lecture can be used to accomplish this.) Students should not be required to take personal notes during this time, but should be watching the overhead projector. Later, the teacher can explain why and how certain information was selected for recording. The teacher also can instruct students in developing abbreviations for use while taking notes. For example, they can use the abbreviations *w/* for *with, no.* for *number,* and so on. Eventually, individual students can take turns being the "note taker" at the overhead projector and receive feedback about their progress from the teacher and other classmates.

Note-Taking Reviews

Both teachers and students should review the notes that students record during lectures. Teachers can periodically collect students' notes after a lecture session and review them and make comments and suggestions for improvements. Suggestions should be concrete and directly apply to the lecture material presented and to the student's recording of that material. Teachers should avoid general statements such as, "You need to

FIGURE 7.1

METHODS TEACHERS CAN USE
TO IMPROVE STUDENTS' NOTE TAKING

||||||||||||||||||||||||||||||||||||||||||||||||||||||||||||||||||||||||||||||||||||||||||||||||||||||||||||||||||

- Make sure you are **not** lecturing too fast.

- Use the board to write key terms, names, definitions, etc.

- Teach students to recognize notetaking cues.

- Provide notetaking cues while lecturing.

- Instruct students in shorthand methods for recording notes.

- Provide skeletal notes and advance organizers.

- Preview information **before** presenting it on transparencies.

- Review students' notes and provide feedback concerning improvement.

- Instruct students in organizing their notes.

take more notes," and instead make specific recommendations, such as, "You should have recorded the causes for crop failures."

Teachers should provide students with several opportunities to review their own notes. For example, after a lecture, they can give students a few minutes to read through their notes and then to ask questions to clarify any missing information or vague recordings.

Students can also take time to review the notes of their peers, discuss any differences with one another, and ask the teacher for clarifications, if necessary. During this time, students also can describe their note-taking strategies to one another.

The day before as well as immmediately prior to exams, students should be given additional opportunities to review their notes.

Organization and Elaboration of Notes

Students should be taught and encouraged not to review their notes in a rote fashion. When reviewing their notes, they should organize the information and classify the ideas recorded (Askov and Kamm 1982). They should be instructed on how to focus on key phrases or vocabulary words as well as on how to relate this information to other information from previous lessons, their textbooks, and classroom demonstrations.

Other Techniques

Several "split-page" or columnar methods have been developed that allow students to organize their notes. One such method is the Directed Note-Taking Activity (DNA) developed by Spires and Stone (1989). DNA is a split-page method that allows students to differentiate between main and supporting ideas. Figure 7.2 provides an example. Using this method, main ideas and concepts are recorded on the left side of the page, and definitions, examples, and supporting details are recorded on the right side. The split-page method not only provides students with a method for organizing their notes but also presents their notes in a manner that facilitates self-testing during study. Students can

FIGURE 7.2

SPLIT-PAGE NOTETAKING
SAMPLE

TOPIC	Classification in science
Classifi-cation	Placing things into groups is classification
Taxonomers	Scientists who classify are called taxonomers
How to Classify	Classification is based on careful observation of differences. Size, shape, and color are differences often used to classify living things.

cover the right column and attempt to recall information recorded there based on the cues in the left column and then check on their accuracy. (See Chapter 5 for self-testing instructions.) For most students, especially beginning note takers, this columnar approach to notes is best accomplished while reviewing notes rather than during the initial recording of notes because of information-processing demands.

DNA is similar to the Cornell System (Pauk 1974) of note taking. In the Cornell System, students take lecture notes in a right-hand column during the actual lecture, and afterward, summarize key words and phrases in a smaller left-hand column. While studying, they can cover the right-hand column and try to recall the information by using the cues in the left-hand column. DNA, however, also involves a self-monitoring or self-questioning component. This component has students ask themselves critical questions *before* ("How interested am I in this topic?"), *during* ("Am I concentrating and paying attention?" "Do I understand the lecture material?"), and *after* the lecture, (Did I accomplish what I set out to do?"). Although Spries and Stone (1989) tested this approach on college freshman only, they believe it would benefit secondary students as well.

Taking Notes While Reading

Not only do many students have difficulty recording effective lecture notes but many are also inadequate recorders of reading notes. These inadequacies occur even though the information-processing demands of transcribing reading notes are usually less than those for lecture notes because: (1) the written text is always available and (2) students can proceed at their own pace. The major problems students have with reading notes are identifying what should be recorded and recording the information in a manner that promotes retention and learning. Examinations of students' reading notes often reveal verbatim copying of material. In fact, Bretzing and Kulhavy (1981) found that high school students took reading notes verbatim from a reading passage even when given instructions to do otherwise. Verbatim copying hinders study because it promotes rote learning and does not encourage students to process the information they are copying.

Garner (1990) describes three developmental stages related to taking notes while processing reading material. She calls students in the first stage *strategically deficient* because they usually make a single pass through the reading material and do not attempt to restate or record any of the information. They have difficulty identifying important information from the reading and usually recall information that is of high interest to them, regardless of the relevance that information has to the passage. In summary, children at this stage of independent reading do little to process text.

Garner describes students in the second stage as *strategically inefficient.* They know they should select and record important information from assigned reading, but they carry out both of these operations in an inefficient manner. Brown and Day (1983) described the independent reading behavior of children in this stage as "copy-delete" because while taking reading notes they make a verbatim copy of the text, they do not paraphrase or summarize information, and they stop taking notes when they run out of space.

Students in Garner's third stage of independent reading are *efficient summarizers.* They select only the important information to summarize. They also use rules for condensing text and will revise or reduce their summaries if necessary. Their summaries of reading material do not include unnecessary information or redundancy, and they select topic sentences or create them if none appears in the text.

The following are three activities the classroom teacher can use to help students become more efficient note takers of reading material.

Cues for Note Taking

Similar to the earlier suggestion for lecture notes, teachers can instruct students in searching for cues, such as underlined or italicized words, headings, questions, pictures and graphs; and for key words or phrases, such as "the reason for . . . ," "an important point . . . ," and so on. Students can then work together in small groups, looking for cues for taking notes from a reading passage. They can compare their results with those from other groups and discuss their differences as well as what cues they used to identify important information to record.

Advance Organizers

Teachers can provide students in advance with cues concerning what is important information to record from text. Called an advance organizer, this technique can take the form of a study guide or set of study questions, a list of words to define, or skeletal notes of the reading assignment for students to complete.

Reading Summaries

Strategies used for reading comprehension and retention can also be used to facilitate note taking. These strategies include the reciprocal teaching strategy described in Chapter 5 and the SQ3R method described in Chapter 6. When using the reciprocal teaching method, teachers can have students actually write down the summaries they must devise; when using SQ3R, they can have students record the answers to the questions they must pose. Students can then review this written material (notes) during study.

READING COMPREHENSION

Students at the secondary level often face more difficult reading and must understand the material much more independently. In addition to the techniques discussed in Chapter 6 for improving reading comprehension, the following may enhance reading comprehension for high school students.

1. The *lookback technique* can be very helpful for students who have difficulty comprehending short stories or other literature. Lookback requires students to: (1) pause after reading a paragraph or whenever necessary; (2) ask themselves questions such as—Who is the main character? What is his/her goal? What is the result of his/her action? How does the story end?; (3) recognize and acknowledge the answers they do not know; and (4) look back in the reading to find those answers (Schewel and Waddell 1986). Students might even keep a journal that physically logs important facts, ideas, and questions (such as: What is the time period? How is that time different from our own? What social, economic, and political events occurred? What was the culture like, the relationship of the sexes, the social classes?). Creating a broad view of the setting makes it easier to retain and recall information.

2. Role playing is a particularly good strategy for improving comprehension when reading a play; it also works well with other literature. Role playing involves becoming a character, reciting lines, acting out behavior, and describing the character's feelings and values. Saying lines or dialogue aloud and moving in action to the work's story line, increases comprehension, relevance, and retention (Woolfolk 1990).

3. Elaboration and personalization strategies (discussed in Chapters 5 and 6) also improve meaningfulness and relevance. Figure 7.3 illustrates how one student made grammar meaningful by placing the terms into humorous newspaper personals!

4. When reading fiction laden with symbolic meaning or when reading nonfiction that presents fairly abstract ideas, students need to think about the implications of each sentence and to use cues (i.e., headings) provided by the authors to aid understanding. The page-break method suggests students read one page at a time and check for comprehension before moving onto the next page. RAP (Ellis and Lenz 1987) is

FIGURE 7.3

USING MNEMONICS TO IMPROVE MEMORY FOR GRAMMAR*

||||||||||||||||||||||||||||||||||||||||||||||||||||||||||||||||||||||||||||||||||||||||||||||||||||||||||||||||||||||

PERSONALS

WANTED: **Single transitive verb** looking for a young, attractive **direct object** that will follow me anywhere. Will take your **determiner.** To make a hot **predictable verb phrase,** call anytime 555/357-411.

WANTED: I'm in a **conditional mood** and am looking for a **modal** to be **present** with me. We **can** go anywhere. I **shall** take good care of you; you **will** like what I have to offer, and we **may** develop a great relationship. Please **precede** me in our next **sentence.**

WANTED: **Nonrestrictive relative clause** free to move to any location in your **sentence.** Will be equal with you at all times. But I know when I'm in the way and will leave without changing your meaning. Believe me, I won't tie you down like that **restrictive** guy.

WANTED: Recently widowed **linking verb** in search of a nice, dependable, sympathetic **noun** or **adjective phrase.** I'm not like those **intransitive verbs** who can stand alone; I need your help. Together we can **rename** our **subject.** There are only a dozen or so of us around, so join me today, and we can make a beautiful **sentence** together.

CLASSIFIED

EMBED ANY PHRASE OR CLAUSE you wish to include in your **complex sentence.** I also take apart the longest of sentences by removing one piece at a time. Call me today for a wide range of **diagrams** explaining my work.

PREPOSITION SERVICE RELATES SENTENCE PARTS. I deliver either one-word or multi-word packages to precede any noun phrase. Note of caution: your new **prepositional phrase** will often act as an **adverb,** so keep its 13 or so functions well in mind when using.

*Written by Heather Coiner while a student at Indiana University of Pennsylvania, English Education Program.

another strategy for making sure you understand a paragraph. Its three steps are: (1) **r**ead a paragraph; (2) **a**sk yourself the main idea and two details; and (3) **p**ut the ideas into your own words.

TEST TAKING

In order to make satisfactory progress in high school, students must acquire not only good study strategies, but also good test-taking skills. Because tests are a reality of our educational system, classroom success frequently depends on the test grades earned by students. When announcing an upcoming test, a teacher may tell students what to study and what type of exam (e.g., multiple choice) to prepare for. During the exam, a teacher may review the test's instructions with the class. The teacher probably will not, however, describe general strategies students can use while taking the test to help raise their test scores. Many teachers assume that students already have acquired not only the skills necessary to prepare correctly for the exam, but also those skills vital for actually taking the test. Students who lack test-taking skills are at a disadvantage.

Many students could become more successful in the classroom if their deficiencies in test-taking skills were remediated. This section reviews general methods (test wiseness) for doing well on exams, discusses the relationship between metacognition and test performance, and suggests methods classroom teachers can use to improve their students' test-taking skills.

Test Wiseness

Although most research on test taking focuses on anxiety, motivation, timed versus untimed tests, and culture-free tests (Rothman and Cohen 1988), some investigations have addressed the issue of raising test scores in general through methods known as *test wiseness*. Test wiseness focuses on using the characteristics of the test and/or test-taking situation to receive a higher score

(Millman, Bishop, and Ebel 1965). Test wiseness is independent of subject-matter knowledge and includes such strategies as time management, guessing, eliminating distractors, careful attention to directions, careful checking of all answers, deductive reasoning, recognition of cues, and considering the intent of question.

For example, Scruggs, Bennion, and Lifson (1985) investigated the test-wiseness strategies used on reading achievement tests by students who represented a wide range of ability levels from grades one through six. These strategies included skipping items, using guessing methods, eliminating inappropriate alternatives, and using external information. The authors also reported that students rarely referred to the reading passage. In fact, in 89 percent of the cases where students answered a question incorrectly, they had not referred to the passage that contained the correct answer. A great deal of carelessness also was observed in attention to distractors. When students answered incorrectly, 40 percent had not read all the distractors. When students answered correctly, they had attended to all distractors in 73 percent of the cases. Clearly, students would profit from instruction in both of these areas.

Several approaches have been used to teach test wiseness to students. Instruction usually focuses on time use, error avoidance, guessing, deductive reasoning, and carelessness (Ligon 1983). Samson (1985) reviewed 24 studies conducted in natural settings that instructed students in test-wiseness skills and found significant improvements in trained children's achievement-test scores. Programs that lasted at least five weeks had a significantly greater impact than did shorter programs. Bangert-Drowns, Kulik, and Kulik (1983) also reported that length of training was related to increased test scores in their meta-analyses of test-taking training. Length of training is also related to developmental level. Scruggs, White, and Bennion (1986) reported that it takes much more training before there are observable benefits for students in first through third grade than for students in fourth through sixth grade.

Ritter and Idol-Maestas (1986) used the acronym SCORER (developed by Carman and Adams, 1972) to teach test-wiseness to middle grade students, some of whom were learning disabled. Training included this advice:

- **S**chedule your time. Students were taught how to estimate the amount of time they should spend on each section of a given exam and told to actually write these estimations in their corresponding areas on the test.

- **C**lue into the right words. Students were taught how to identify clue words and then told to underline them in the test's instructions.

- **O**mit difficult questions. Students were taught to mark difficult questions with "+" or "++" so they could later return to these.

- **R**ead carefully. Students were taught to read test directions and test items carefully.

- **E**stimate your answer. Students were taught to place an "e" next to any item they felt they might answer incorrectly.

- **R**eview. Students were taught to review a test before turning it in, and indicate they had reviewed it by writing an "R" at the top of the exam.

Metacognition and Test Monitoring

Metacognition, as defined previously, is knowledge about one's own cognitive activity (Siegler 1991). Metacognition that controls ongoing thinking is important and includes at least three components (Pressley et al. 1987): *planning* or figuring out how to proceed on a task; *predicting* or estimating how well one will do or how long a task will take; and *monitoring* or checking whether or not a goal has been reached. There are opportunities for all three of these during testing. Previous test performance can be used to plan restudy of material. Predictions about future academic performance depends in part on awareness of one's own past test performance. Knowledge about performance that is gained through monitoring test performance can be an important determinant of whether students realize that more study is necessary to accomplish a goal.

Test monitoring is an area of study that measures students' metacognitions about current or future exam performance. Students either estimate their performance on test items just completed or predict how they will perform on future items. Research indicates that test monitoring develops over the course of elementary school. For example, Pressley et al. (1987) found that children in grades four and five were more accurate in their estimations of their actual exam performance than were children in first and second grade. The authors also reported that boys were more optimistic about their performance on individual items, especially on those items they answered incorrectly, than were girls. Other investigators also have found boys to be more self-assured when taking a test than girls (Pressley and Ghatala 1989; Whitley, McHugh, and Frieze 1986). Pressley and Ghatala (1989) reported that when seventh and eighth grade students took a hard test, they lowered their expectations about future performance. They did not change their expectations, however, when they took an easy test. Test experience did not have the same influence on first and second grade children. Their predictions were affected little by taking a test. Pressley and Ghatala (1989) concluded that children in grades seven and eight have developed skills to monitor performance on test items and to recognize that current performance predicts future outcomes; first and second grade children have not developed these skills.

Young children (i.e., grades one and two) have not had much formal experience with academic exams and are not as aware as older children are of how they are doing on exams. Teaching test monitoring to young children is painstaking, however, involving explicit instruction about all aspects of the monitoring process and how monitoring relates to future performance (Ghatala et al. 1986). Pressley and Ghatala (1989) suggest that because test monitoring seems well developed by

141

grades seven and eight in most children, it makes sense to defer efforts aimed at encouraging the use of metacognitive information gained from testing until the middle grades. Classroom teachers in the elementary grades can, however, provide the specific metacognitive knowledge to be gained from test taking directly to their students. For example, the teacher can tell students when an upcoming exam will be more difficult than usual and will require more study. The teacher can also point out to students their individual testing-taking strengths and weaknesses (and provide concrete methods for remediation).

Suggestions to Improve Test-Taking Skills

Students can improve their test-taking skills. As mentioned earlier, however, this requires repeated instruction and reminders about such activities. The following activities are ones classroom teachers can use to improve the test-taking skills of their students. Figures 7.4 and 7.5 also provide guidelines for students who are preparing for and taking a test, respectively.

1. *Take practice tests.* Practice questions and practice tests provide opportunities for testing experience and remediation. Unfortunately, teachers rarely use sample tests or sample test-questions with students (Rothman and Cohen 1988). Practice tests provide students with an opportunity to practice their test-taking skills. They also provide teachers with feedback about individual students' test-taking strengths and weaknesses. Teachers can offer students practice tests and sample test questions and allow adequate time for class discussion of the test-taking strategies they used and the results they received. The guidelines described in Figures 7.4 and 7.5 can also be practiced and discussed.

2. *Analyze incorrect answers.* One way of remediating students' test-taking abilities is to identify why students answered specific items incorrectly. This analysis is essential if students

FIGURE 7.4

GUIDELINES FOR PREPARING FOR A TEST

‖‖

1. **Know when the test will be given**—what date, time, etc. Will you have the entire class period to complete the exam, or will it be given at the beginning or end of class? Will this be a timed test?

2. **Know what the test will cover**—what chapters, notes, etc. Will you be asked to apply information to new situations not specifically discussed in class or in the textbook?

3. **Know your teacher.** Would your teacher give detailed questions about specific dates, numbers, distances, or names? Will your teacher allow you to ask questions concerning words you do not understand? Will you be allowed to ask how to interpret a question? Will your teacher allow you to use external aids such as dictionaries, tables, and calculators while taking the test? Ask your teacher these and other questions **before** the test date.

4. **Know what kind of test you will be taking**—fill-in-the-blank, completion, essay, multiple-choice, or true/false questions?

5. **Know how to study.** Which study methods will work best for the material you need to learn and the type of test you will be given? Plan your study ahead of time so you will have ample opportunity to learn all the material. Do **not** cram at the last minute. Ask yor teacher for suggestions about studying. While studying, predict material or questions that are likely to be on the test.

6. **Know yourself.** What are you test-taking strengths and weaknesses? What type of questions or types of material are most difficult for you? Plan methods that overcome your weaknesses and capitalize on your strengths. Ask your teacher for suggestions. Remember, rest, proper nutrition, and exercise are important for good test performance.

7. See **GUIDELINES FOR TAKING A TEST**, Figure 7.5

FIGURE 7.5

GUIDELINES FOR TAKING A TEST*

|||||||||||||||||||||||||||||||||||||||||||||||||||||||||||||||||||||||||||||||||||||||||||||||||||||||||||||||||||||||||||

1. Take time to read test directions carefully before answering the questions. Watch for changes in directions.

2. Skim or look over the entire test before you begin answering individual questions.

3. Do not read more into a question than is actually there.

4. Place a question mark in front of any question you are uncertain about rather then spend too much time on it. Return to this question after you have answered the other questions. Eliminate the obvious incorrect answers when responding to multiple-choice questions.

5. For items that are difficult to answer, underline key words.

6. Read all choices before making a selection on a multiple-choice exam.

7. Look for absolute words such as "all," "none," "never," "always"; keep in mind there are few absolutes in our world.

8. All parts of a true/false question must be true before the statement can be true.

9. When matching, first answer items that are known and then go back to remaining items and make the best choices.

10. Always proofread your test before turning it in. If you have time, go back and reconsider all your answers.

11. Never change an answer unless you understand clearly why you are doing so.

12. Ignore the pace of other students.

*Adapted from Schilling 1984

are to improve upcoming performances. Incorrect answers fall into several possible categories (Rothman and Cohen 1988).

Lack of Information: A student may have answered incorrectly because the student never learned the material. Questioning can determine if this lack of learning occurred because of poor study habits, poor note-taking skills, inattention, and so on.

Carelessness: Carelessness can occur because a student was hasty and did not read or listen to the directions for taking the test, answered without careful reading, or ignored relevant information.

Misinterpretation: Misinterpretation is a problem with processing language. If a student cannot interpret the meaning of a question, she or he will not be able to answer correctly. Rothman and Cohen (1988) suggest that one way to help students process language on exams is to allow them to read the questions aloud to themselves. Another way is to encourage students to ask questions if they are unsure about directions or wording of questions.

Material Not Studied: This is a problem when too little material or incorrect material was studied for the exam. This may have occurred because the student misinterpreted the teacher's instructions concerning what the exam would cover.

Incorrect Reading: Incorrect answers on an exam are frequently linked to decoding errors. Methods to help students improve their decoding skills (see Chapter 5) will help both reading comprehension and test-taking skills. When appropriate, students should be encouraged to seek assistance with words they cannot decode.

3. *Outline answers.* Often, students begin to answer an essay question and then drift away from what the question asks and

as a result, lose critical points from their tests scores. When answering an essay question, an outline helps students organize and focus their thinking. Students should be instructed in writing outlines before beginning their written responses to essay questions. During testing, students should be reminded and encouraged to use the outline method. Teachers may even require that students turn in their outlines for test credit (or extra credit).

4. *Examine test-taking skills in groups.* While in small groups, students can: (a) identify and discuss common study and test-taking problems, (b) evaluate their own study habits and attitudes, (c) create a profile of their own test-taking strengths and weaknesses, and (d) discuss and develop solutions to their test-taking problems (Wilson 1986).

5. *Use textbooks.* Schilling (1984) suggests that at the end of tests, teachers give students five minutes to use their textbooks or notes to search for answers they are unsure of. This requires planning and judgments concerning which questions deserve this time and also requires students to use their knowledge of their textbooks, notes, and indexes.

Remembering Information for Tests

At the high school level, students must encode, retrieve, and understand more verbatim material than ever before. Remembering vocabulary for exams may be especially difficult. Word identification can always be better achieved when mnemonic devices are used. In many cases, definitions of words can be more easily remembered when paired with a similar, more familiar word with the same first letter. For example, the word *miscible* (meaning "can mix in any proportion") can be remembered by thinking of *mixable* ("mixable in any proportion"), Miscible = Mixable (Deshler and Shumaker 1986).

DISSECT is another strategy that is useful for understanding difficult or long vocabulary words. The steps in

DISSECT include: (1) discovering the context, (2) isolating the prefix, (3) separating the suffix, (4) saying the stem, (5) examining the stem by using the "rule of twos and threes"—if it begins with a vowel remove two letters, if it begins with a consonant remove three, (6) checking with someone, and (7) trying the dictionary. Say the term *isobutanol* is being compared to normal-butanol, (one could then expect the same elements but in different order), the prefix is *iso-*, the suffix is *-ol* as in *alcohol*, the stem is *butan*, applying the rule of three the stem is "but" meaning four. Now we know that there are four carbons; we know that it is an alcohol, and we know that it is not normal-butanol. By using step six or seven the actual chemical reaction can be found (Gage and Berliner 1992).

When trying to distinguish between two terms, the paired associate method (pairing the new term with an old, already known term) works well. Alphabetical associate pairing, for example, is successful for students trying to remember the difference between anions and cations. One is positive while one is negative. Anions are negative; cations are positive. Because *a* comes before *c*, and *n* comes before *p*, anions can be remembered as negative and cations as positive (Deshler and Shumaker 1986).

When students have a large amount of information to organize and recall, the CANDO strategy (Ellis and Lenz 1987) helps them to take gradual steps and divide their learning into parts they can handle. The steps include: (1) creating a list, (2) asking if the list is complete, (3) noting main ideas, (4) describing each component, and (5) overlearning. As in all strategy instruction, the MIRRORS teaching method described in Figure 5.1 (Chapter 5) should be used. Even at the high school level, students often require intensive training before they will adopt study or learning strategies spontaneously.

CONCLUSION

Teaching test-taking skills, memorization, comprehension, and note-taking skills should be an ongoing process in the classroom. Teachers should not teach to the test but should teach students how to study and take tests so they will be prepared for current as well as future learning situations. There are some commercially prepared packages that help students learn test-taking skills. The Wilson (1986) article described earlier is one, and the *Test-Taking Skills Kit* (1980) is another. Figure 3.1 (see Chapter 3) provides others. Most importantly, teachers should encourage high school students to develop a personal learning system that includes an effective note-taking system, an automatic strategy for improving comprehension and recognizing confusion when reading, a plan of study that adapts for type of test and depth of knowledge required when studying for a test, and a strong repertoire of mnemonic devices. These are the skills of the independent learner, and they are as essential for success outside the classroom as are basic reading and writing skills. It's about time we start teaching them.

REFERENCES

Annis, L.S., and Davis, J.K. "Effects of Encoding and External Memory Device on Note Taking." *Journal of Experimental Education* 44 (1975): 44–46.

————. "A Normative Study of Students' Reported Preferred Study Techniques." *Reading World* 21 (1982): 201–07.

Askov, B., and Kamm, K. *Study Skills in the Content Areas.* Boston: Allyn and Bacon, 1982.

Bangert-Drowns, R.L., Kulik, J.A., and Kulik, C.C. "Effects of Coaching on Achievement Test Performance." *Review of Educational Research* 53 (1983): 571–85.

Bretzing, B.H., and Kulhavy, R.W. "Note-Taking and Passage Style." *Journal of Educational Psychology* 73 (1981): 242–50.

Brezting, B.H., Kulhavy, R.W., and Caterino, L.C. "Note Taking by Junior High Students." *Journal of Educational Research* 80 (1987): 359–62.

Brown, A.L., Bransford, J.D., Ferrara, R.A., and Campione, J.C. "Learning, Remembering, and Understanding." In *Handbook of Child*

Psychology (Vol. 3), edited by J. H. Flavell and E. M. Markman. New York: Wiley, 1983.

Brown, A.L., and Day, J.D. "Macrorules for Summarizing Texts: The Development of Expertise." *Journal of Verbal Learning and Verbal Behavior* 22 (1983): 1–14.

Carman, R.A., and Adams, W.R. *Study Skills: A Student's Guide for Survival.* New York: Wiley, 1972.

Castallo, R. "Listening Guide—A First Step Toward Note Taking and Listening Skills." *Journal of Reading* 19 (1976): 289–90.

Collingwood, V., and Hughes, D.C. "The Effects of Three Types of University Lecture Notes on Student Achievement." *Journal of Educational Psychology* 70 (1978): 175–79.

Cook, L.K., and Mayer, R.E. "Reading Strategies Training for Meaningful Learning from Prose." In *Cognitive Strategy Research: Educational Applications*, edited by M. Pressley and J.R. Levin. New York: Springer Verlag, 1983.

Deshler, D.D., and Shumaker, J.B. "Learning Strategies: An Instructional Alternative for Low Achieving Adolescents." *Exceptional Children* 52 (1986): 583–90.

DiVesta, F.J., and Gray, G.S. "Listening and Note Taking." *Journal of Educational Psychology* 63 (1972): 8–14.

Einstein, G.O., Morris, J., and Smith, S. "Note Taking, Individual Differences, and Memory for Lecture Information." *Journal of Educational Psychology* 77 (1985): 522–32.

Ellis, E.S., and Lenz, B.K. "A Component Analysis of Effective Learning Strategies for LD Students." *Learning Disabilities Focus* 2 (1987): 94–107.

Estes, W.K. *Handbook of Learning and Cognitive Processes, Attention, and Memory* (Vol. 4). Hillsdale, N.J.: Lawrence Erlbaum, 1976.

Gage, N.L., and Berliner, D.C. *Educational Psychology* (5th edition). Boston: Houghton Mifflin, 1992.

Garner, R. "Children's Use of Strategies in Reading." In *Children's Strategies: Contemporary Views of Cognitive Development*, edtied by D.F. Bjorklund. Hillsdale, N.J.: Erlbaum, 1990.

Ghatala, E.S., Levin, J.R., Pressley, M., and Goodwin, D. "A Componential Analysis of the Effects of Derived and Supplied Strategy-Utility Information on Children's Strategy Selections." *Journal of Experimental Child Psychology* 41 (1986): 76–92.

Hartley, J. "Lecture Handouts and Student Note-Taking." *Programmed Learning and Educational Technology* 13 (1976): 58–64.

Hartley, J. and Cameron, A. "Some Observations on the Efficiency of Lecturing." *Educational Review* 20 (1967): 30–37.

Kiewra, K. A. "Students' Note-Taking Behaviors and the Efficacy of Providing the Instructor's Notes for Review." *Contemporary Educational Psychology* 10 (1985): 378–86.

————. "Providing the Instructor's Notes: An Effective Addition to Student Note-Taking." *Educational Psychologist* 20 (1985): 33–39.

Kiewra, K.A., and Fletcher, H.J. "The Relationship Between Levels of Note Taking and Achievement." *Human Learning* 3 (1984): 273–80.

Kiewra, K.A., and Frank, B.M. "Encoding and External Storage Effects of Personal Lecture Notes, Skeletal Notes, and Detailed Notes for Field-Independent Learners." *Journal of Educational Research* 81 (1988): 143–48.

Ladas, H. "Summarizing Research: A Case Study." *Review of Educational Research* 50 (1980): 597–624.

Ligon, G. "Preparing Students for Standardized Testing." *New Directions for Testing and Measurement* 19 (1983): 19–27.

Maddox, H., and Laughran, R.J. "Illustrating the Lecture: Prepared Diagrams vs. Built-up Diagrams." *Audio Visual Communication Review* 25 (1977): 87–90.

McAndrew, D.A. "Underlining and Note Taking: Some Suggestions from Research." *Journal of Reading* 27 (1983): 103–08.

Millman, J., Bishop, C.H., and Ebel, R. "An Analysis of Test Wiseness." *Psychological Measurement* 25 (1965): 707–26.

Norton, L.S. "The Effects of Note Taking and Subsequent Use on Long-term Recall." *Programmed Learning and Educational Technology* 18 (1981): 16–22.

Palkovitz, R.J., and Lore, R.K. "Note Taking and Note Review: Why Students Fail Questions Based on Lecture Material." *Teaching of Psychology* 7 (1980): 159–61.

Palmaiter, R.A., and Bennett, M.J. "Note-Taking Habits of College Students." *Journal of Reading* 18 (1974): 215–18.

Pauk, W. *How to Study in College* (2nd edition). Boston: Houghton, Mifflin, 1974.

Pressley, M., and Ghatala, E.S. "Metacognitive Benefits of Taking a Test for Children and Young Adolescents." *Journal of Experimental Child Psychology* 47 (1989): 430–50.

Pressley, M., Levin, J.R., Ghatala, E.S., and Ahmad, M. "Test Monitoring in Young Grade School Children." *Journal of Experimental Child Psychology* 43 (1987): 96–111.

Risch, N.L., and Kiewra, K.A. "Content and Form Variations in Note-Taking: Effects Among Junior High Students." *Journal of Educational Research* 83 (1990): 355–57.

Ritter, S., and Idol-Maestas, L. "Teaching Middle School Students to Use a Test-Taking Strategy." *Journal of Educational Research* 79 (1986): 350–57.

Rothman, R.W., and Cohen, J. "Teaching Test-Taking Skills." *Academic Therapy* 23 (1988): 341–48.

Samson, G.E. "Effects of Training in Test-Taking Skills on Achievement Test Performance: A Quantitative Synthesis." *Journal of Educational Research* 78 (1985): 261–66.

Saski, J., Swicegood, P., and Carter, J. "Note-Taking Formats for Learning Disabled Adolescents." *Learning Disability Quarterly* 6 (1983): 265–72.

Schewel, R.H., and Waddell, J.G. "Metacognitive Skills: Practical Strategies." *Academic Therapy* 22 (1986): 19–25.

Schilling, F.C. "Teaching Study Skills in the Intermediate Grades—We Can Do More." *Journal of Reading* 28 (1984): 620–23.

Scruggs, T.E., Bennion, K., and Lifson, S. "An Analysis of Children's Strategy Use on Reading Achievement Tests." *The Elementary School Journal* 86 (1985): 479–84.

Scruggs, T.E., White, K.R., and Bennion, K. "Teaching Test-Taking Skills to Elementary Grade Students: A Meta-analysis." *The Elementary School Journal* 87 (1986): 69–82.

Sheinker, J., and Sheinker, A. *Study Strategies: A Metacognitive Approach.* Roch Springs, Wy.: White Mountain, 1982.

Siegler, R.S. *Children's Thinking* (2nd edition). Englewood Cliffs, N.J.: Prentice Hall, 1991.

Spires, H.A., and Stone, D.P. "The Directed Note-Taking Activity: A Self-Questioning Approach." *Journal of Reading* 32 (1989): 36–39.

Test-Taking Skills Kit. Herndon, Vir.: Evaluation and Assessment Service, 1980.

Whitley, B.E., Jr., McHugh, M.C., and Frieze, I.H. "Assessing the Theoretical Models for Sex Differences in Causal Attributions of Success and Failure." *The Psychology of Gender: Advances Through*

Meta-analysis, edited by J.S. Hyde and M.C. Linn. Baltimore, Md: Johns Hopkins Press, 1986.

Wilson, N.S. "Preparing for Examinations: A Classroom Guidance Unit." *The School Counselor* 33 (1986): 297–305.

Woolfolk, A. *Educational Psychology*, (4th edition). Englewood Cliffs, N.J.: Prentice Hall, 1990.